SHORT WALKS FOR MOTORISTS

SHORT WALKS for Motorists
24 Pennine Walks around Todmorden
with Geoff Boswell

ISBN 0 9510790 1 8
First Edition 1990

Also by Geoff Boswell: On the Tops around Todmorden.

Published by: Delta G, Hollinroyd Farm, Butts Lane,
Todmorden, OL14 8RJ. Tel. (0706) 813860

Text prepared by author on a BBC Microcomputer
using the Scribe word processing program.
Text transferred directly from disc and photo typeset by:
Koinonia Limited, Bury Business Centre, Bury, Lancs.

Printed by: The Arc and Throstle Press,
Nanholme Mill, Shaw Wood Road,
Todmorden, OL14 6DA.

Cover photograph: Walking up to Langfield Edge (Walk 1)
overloooking Horse Wood, Lumbutts and Mankinholes.

SHORT WALKS
for Motorists

24 Pennine Walks around Todmorden
with
Geoff Boswell

Delta G
Todmorden

For Ann

Contents

Acknowledgements

My thanks are due to many people who have helped with this book. My wife Ann pursuaded me to write it and walked most of the routes to ensure that they were really short, easy and realistically timed. The extensions to Walks 10 and 15 do not come in this category and carry appropriate warnings!

Colin and Margaret Wright often accompanied us in our exploration of the Pennine countryside and added laughter to the occasion.

Brian and Jeanne Clatworthy and their children Joanna, Elizabeth and David, who waited patiently for the heat haze of 1989 to lift so that I could photograph them for the cover.

My thanks to are due to Wilf Sutcliffe, Footpaths secretary of the Calderdale branch of the Ramblers' Association for his interest, proof reading and welcome information on Blake Dean Railway.

Thanks to the staff of Todmorden Information Centre for their proof reading and useful comments.

Finally to Mary Cockcroft and my wife Ann for careful proof reading - any remaining errors are mine.

Introduction

This little volume was written in response to some readers of my earlier book "On the Tops around Todmorden" who declared that walks of nine to twenty six miles were far too long! Could I provide a book of shorter walks that might suit families with children, or perhaps older people who just enjoy an easy stroll in beautiful scenery, and who like to read of the history and folk lore of places they visit?

All the walks in this book are within the area of the South Pennines Leisure Map, published by the Ordnance Survey. This covers a range of low hills and valleys which cross the Yorkshire/Lancashire border. Although the administration of the Pennine area is divided between many local authorities, the South Pennines share a common heritage and a geography which gives the area a unity. The Pennines are a wild, beautiful space between the counties, admirably suited for walking and relaxation.

The two River Calders arise in these hills. One eventually flows into the Irish Sea, the other into the North Sea. The rivers have forged deep valleys since the last ice age. Along the sides of the valleys trees abound. Above the valleys lies an agricultural plain of enclosed land before the untamed hills take off into open moorland where the grouse is still king. It is an area which has a rich heritage of rural history and industry. Any remaining mill chimneys no longer belch smoke. The gritstone houses are gradually being cleaned, making the area, lovely to live in, with a wide open space for the visitor to enjoy.

The Motorway system almost surrounds the South Pennines but it has not penetrated the heartland. The trans-Pennine M62 runs along its southern edge. On the western side, the M66 runs from Manchester to Accrington joining the M65 which forms the northern boundary, together with the new Kendal to Doncaster trunk road running down the Aire Valley. To the east the M606 is a spur off the M62 running to Bradford. The Motorway box around the South Pennines makes for accessibilty. A twenty minute drive from any one of these motorways will take you deep into the heart of the hills where you can enjoy so many walks and a breath of fresh air. I well remember when I lived in Manchester, long before the M62 was built, and had managed to find the Shepherd's Rest Inn high above Todmorden. To fill one's lungs with clean Pennine air was a joy that has never left me.

The walks are all circular and have been selected for their scenic or historical interest. There length varies from just over one mile to nearly six miles. Many are close to one of the delightful Inns which can provide food and non-alcoholic drinks as well as the usual fare. Sketch maps are provided throughout the book, these give a rough outline of the route but they are no substitute for a proper Ordnance Survey Map. These sketches are not to scale and the scale varies within a sketch. A circular walk of 3 miles may occupy more space on the page than 5 miles of directions to the start point from the motorway. The sketch defines the route and shows all turning points. Readers are strongly advised to get a copy of the South Pennine Leisure Map, scale 1:25000, to locate all the start points from map references listed in the text. Instructions at the base of the map show you how to read map references. All the rights of way are marked on the map in green.

Although the walks are short, they should not be attempted unprepared. Walking boots or stout shoes are essential. Most families can not afford to keep changing boots for growing children and my children ran all over these hills in wellies. Take waterproofs with you. A rain storm can sweep into a valley in minutes, although if you are on the tops then you can usually see it coming. If trouble strikes, and you have left a note in your car saying which walk you are on, you can soon be found. It is very necessary to take this precaution in winter, when the days are short. Even though winter walking on frozen ground is often better than summer walking, it is easy to freeze to death if you are caught in a blizzard. An orange polythene survival bag costs so little and can be a life-saver. If you are caught in a blizzard, seek the shelter of a wall or rock close to your route, don't go wandering off, hopefully the Moorland Rescue teams will soon find you.

Please follow the Country Code. If you want to take a dog with you keep it on a lead when sheep are around, particularly at lambing time. Close all gates, and do take care not to start a fire. Moorland fires can burn for weeks, destroying trees and vegetation. If you are enjoying a picnic or a canned drink, it is easy enough to take the empties home, leaving the hills clean.

Paragraphs which are inset, and in a different type face, contain historical or other information which is not needed in the route description, so these can be omitted when outdoors.

The network of Information Centres throughout the South Pennines provides an excellent service to the day visitor. As well as a good collection of books and postcards, you can get information on local museums, shops, markets, mill shops and garden centres. Country Parks, Visitor Centres and Nature Reserves in the area. They are producing new inexpensive leaflets each year. The telephone number of Todmorden Information Centre is (0706) 818181.

A word or two about parking. Where possible the start points are located on public long stay car parks. Sometimes the start is close to a moorland pub, where there are usually people about to keep an eye on your car. It is best not to use pub car parks unless you intend to use their facilities. Don't leave valuables in the car unless they are out of sight. Finally remember to leave a note in your saying where you have gone: "Short Walks for Motorists No. 24" will do. Then if anything goes amiss the rescue services have your intended route.

Walk No 1
Langfield Common.

Distance 3 miles. Walking time 90 minutes.
Refreshments: The Shepherd's Rest Inn is at the start and end.

Start point: The Shepherd's Rest Inn, Lumbutts Road, Todmorden, Map Reference SD 945232, marked Hey Head Green, on the South Pennine Leisure Map.

Approaches to the start by car. From the south follow the A 6033 from Littleborough to Todmorden and take the right fork at Walsden Post Office. This is a quarter of a mile past the Garden Centre. By car from Todmorden, take the Halifax Road, A 646, until the road goes over a low hill, Castle Hill, and take the first right, opposite the Rose and Crown Inn. At the next T junction turn right and drive for half a mile.

From Halifax and Hebden Bridge. About three miles after Hebden Bridge, on the A 646, look out for picnic site sign at Lobb Mill, pass the site, go round a bend and turn left up Woodhouse Road opposite the Rose and Crown. Follow the road through the wood turning right at the top to the Shepherd's Rest.

Walking from Todmorden, via Fielden Square, Longfield Road, Far Longfield Farm and Lumbutts Road. There is a rather infrequent bus service from Todmorden, the Mankinholes circular, which passes the Shepherd's Rest.

Go through the gate, opposite the Shepherd's Rest, onto Langfield Common. Count 50 paces and look both right and left to pick out the line of the old Causey stones. This was once a route from Halifax to Rochdale and we will meet it again later in this walk.

Continue ahead, taking the higher path which climbs gently towards Langfield Edge. If you accidentally get on the lower path, called Withins New Road, which follows the wall above Horse Wood Farm, you can cut up to the correct path as soon as you reach the wall.

The steady climb gives fine views across the agricultural plain on the edge of the valley. Soon you can see the twin dams above Lumbutts Mill, half left. The square tower of the mill once contained three water wheels generating 54 horse power. Keep to the path as you go, the top soil is thin here and soil erosion can soon set in.

You pass old stone base plates which were part of an overhead ropeway carrying stone from the quarry above down to the road. As you reach the

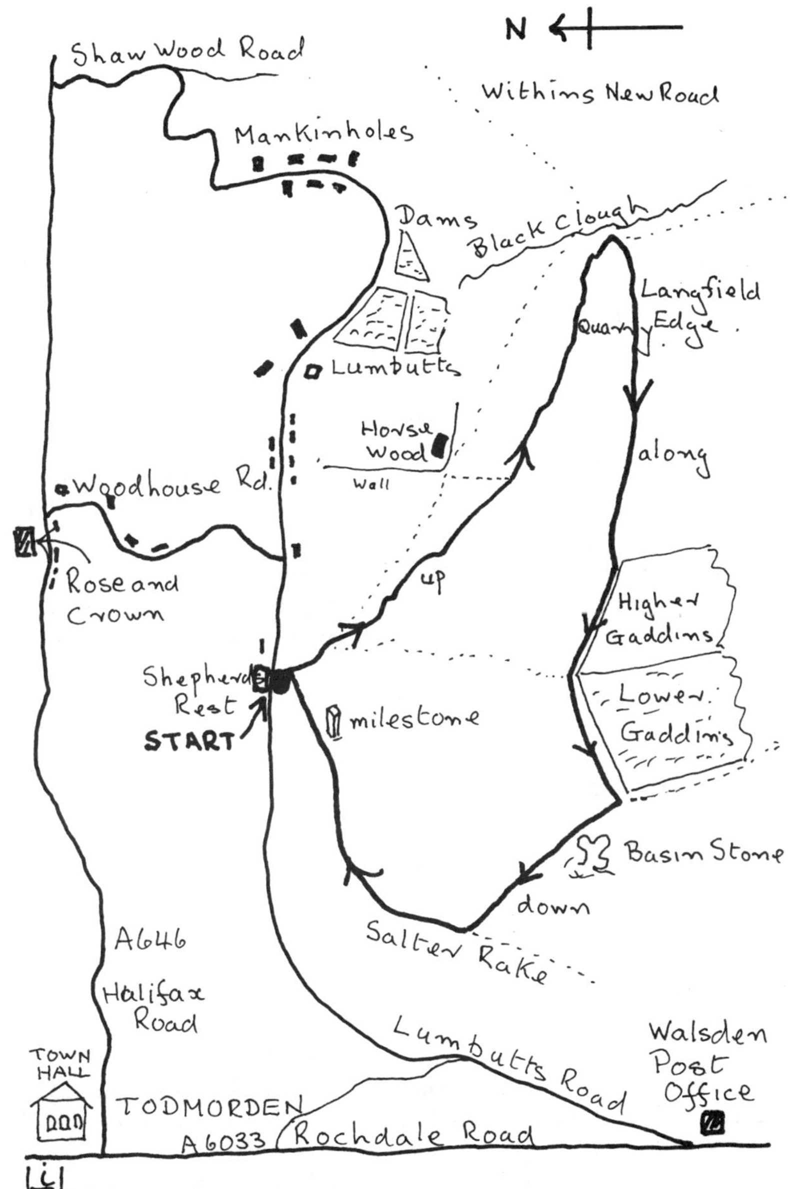
N
Shaw Wood Road
Withins New Road
Mankinholes
Dams
Black Clough
Langfield
Quarry
Edge
Lumbutts
Horse wood
Wall
along
Woodhouse Rd.
Rose and Crown
up
Higher Gaddins
Shepherd's Rest
START
milestone
Lower Gaddins
Basin Stone
down
Salter Rake
A646
Halifax Road
Lumbutts Road
Walsden Post Office
TOWN HALL
TODMORDEN
A6033 Rochdale Road

brow of a hill, the line of Withins New Road can be seen climbing the hill, half left ahead. This was built last century as a coach road, but it is now in a poor state due to landslip and the partial loss of a beautiful bridge across Black Clough. (A chance for some bridleway restoration here.)

If the path appears to divide, it is best to take the lower route to avoid landslip ahead. You soon cross a raised section of road which is close to the site of a spring that supplies the whole of Lumbutts Village with clear sparkling water, straight out of the base of the rocks on your right. The path then narrows and clings to the steeper hillside, as it climbs to an old quarry, with the remains of a quarryman's hut and his fire place standing proud.

Soon, the stream in Black Clough, appears to be coming up to meet you. Be ready to turn sharp right, as soon as you have no rocks on your right, when you have reached Langfield Edge. Follow the path along the edge above the quarries. Parents will need to hold on to children here, particularly if it is windy.

Within minutes you see an old stone slab bridge, on your left across a gully. This is an aqueduct which brought water stored in Higher Gaddings Reservoir ahead, back to the stream in Black Clough, which in turn conveyed it to the water wheels at Lumbutts Mill. This is a form of energy storage now copied in modern pump storage schemes for power stations at Dinorwic in Wales and by the Scottish Hydro-electric Board.

At the second bridge you have reached the controlled outflow of the Higher Gaddings reservoir. It is worth having a look at the old water inlet, some 13 paces into the dam on your left. These deep goits go for miles along the edge of the moor, collecting water. They are now dry because the more recent Warland Drain catches the water higher up and takes it to Warland reservoir.

This was built to supply water to Long Lees Lock at the summit of the trans-Pennine Rochdale Canal. Rochdale Corporation used Warland reservoir for drinking water but now it belongs to the North West Water Authority, who are modernising the supply. Soon Warland will no longer be needed for drinking water and hopefully it will revert to its original use to feed the restored canal.

From the water outlet follow the wall north-west towards Todmorden and Lower Gaddings, which has both water and a small sandy beach. This has been the site of an organised swim on New Years Day. Continue to the next corner, where it is possible to take a short cut back to the Shepherd's Rest by going down the steps and following a path which descends steeply.

However, it really is worth following the bank to the next steps 200 yards further on. Please use the 21 steps and not the bank. If feet and soil erosion continue to wash the bank away one could foresee that the wall could be breached and then a rush of water downhill could cause disaster below.

Follow the path for a few minutes, looking ahead to Basin Stone, a natural pulpit used by both the Chartists and William Holt, one of Todmorden's Authors, who was much concerned with the depression of the 1930s. On the top of the stone there is a bowl, still called locally, "t Devil's Bowl" caused by the wind swirling rainwater around to form a hollow in the gritstone.

The path continues downhill, keeping 100 yards to the left of old boundary markers, which look like stone gateposts stuck on the moor. About ten minutes walk from Basin Stone you suddenly see the line of Causey stones crossing your path at right angles. Turn right along these stones. This is Salter Rake, one of the longest continuous stretches of Causey stones in the Pennines, a treasure which must be preserved. You can help by walking on the line of the stones, rather than to the side.

At the brow of Salter Rake, looking to the left, there is a favourite view over Higher Knowl Farm with the inter-folding hills up Midgelden Valley as a background. Follow the path towards Stoodley Pike, eventually passing between two walls. Look out for the very old milestone standing on your right, with distances to Halifax, Rochdale and Todmorden, before returning to the start.

Walk No 2.
Widdop.

Distance 2.5 miles. Walking time 75 minutes.
Refreshments: The Packhorse Inn, Widdop, south of start.

Start point: Widdop Reservoir, between Heptonstall and Colne. Map Reference SD 936238, marked Widdop Reservoir on the South Pennine Leisure Map. Binoculars and a bird identification book will enhance your enjoyment on this walk.

Approaches to the start by car. From Manchester take the M62 to Junction 21 and proceed via Milnrow, Littleborough and Todmorden as shown on Map 11. At Todmorden turn right and follow the A646 towards Halifax for four miles. Bear left at the lights to Heptonstall and Slack, see Map 5. Follow the main road to the village of Slack. This is easily recognised be the wide grass verges along the road. Bear right at the end of the village, by the old Mount Zion Chapel, and follow the road for about four miles to Widdop, passing the bridge at Blake Dean and the Packhorse Inn. Stop about a mile further on where the power line crosses the road.

From Halifax follow signs to Lancashire and Burnley until you reach Hebden Bridge. Just after the second lights look out for the turning circle to Heptonstall on the left, see Map 5. Turn back along the road you have just come, bear left at the lights. Follow the road to Slack and continue to Widdop as in the last paragraph.

From Lancashire leave the M65 at Junction 12 and follow the A56 back towards Burnley for half a mile to the lights at Brierfield.

Turn left and go one and a half miles to Haggate where you turn left again for Thursden. Another mile or so brings you to a minor road on your right, signed to Hebden Bridge. Now you are really in the Pennines! The road climbs and winds until you see the wild majesty of the Widdop Valley open up before you. Follow the road to the far end of the reservoir before you park your car.

Take the path on the left of the turret-topped wall towards the reservoir dam. The track across the top is a bridleway called Gorple Road. Gorple was an old hamlet now long deserted. We circle the reservoir in a clockwise direction. Rising above the far end of the dam are Widdop rocks, a favourite place for rock climbers.

There is a curious free stone, which looks rather like a sheep from the dam, perched on top of Cludders stack. From other angles it looks more like a tea pot. At the end of the dam turn right past the valve house, in the

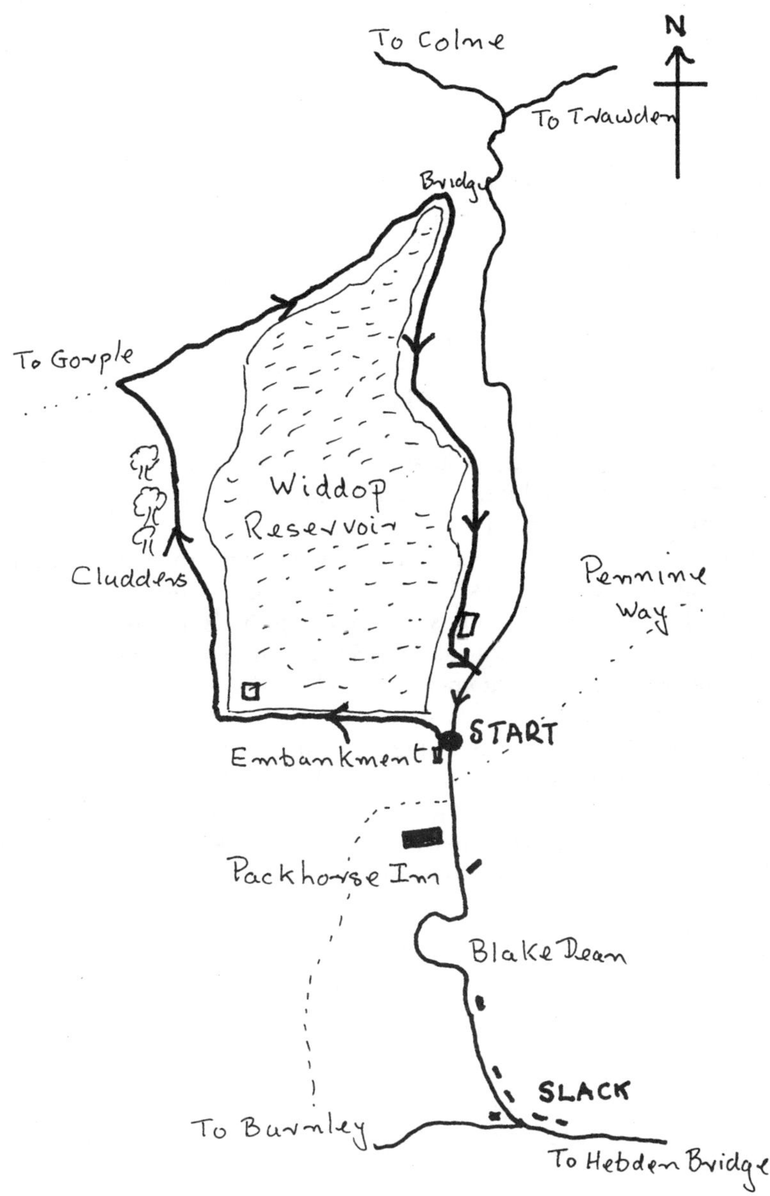
N
To Colne
To Trawden
Bridge
To Gorple
Widdop
Reservoir
Cludders
Pennine
Way
START
Embankment
Packhorse Inn
Blake Dean
SLACK
To Burnley
To Hebden Bridge

style of an Egyptian mausoleum, and follow the track as it rises past the conifer wood.

> Moorland birds will be in full song. In summer the skylarks chirp away, the curlews are easily recognised by their cry, curved bill and brown plumage with flashes of white underneath. This is also the summer haunt of the ring ouzel, rather like a big blackbird with flashes of white, which often perches prominently. Little wheat ears flit across the low ground. An experienced bird watcher may easily spot thirty different species around here. If you are lucky you can see merlin, Britain's smallest bird of prey, or perhaps a dipper down by a stream, or a pied flycatcher sitting on a wall warily watching you.

Where the path forks take the left fork to the higher ground. When you are well up the hill the bridleway takes a sharp right turn across a stream and a signpost comes into view. At the sign, turn right and follow the wall. The view is really good. Here you are in a hidden valley, with a beautiful lake, surrounded by wild moors and the only house in sight is Widdop Lodge across the reservoir in the distance.

Soon the path descends towards the moorland road to Lancashire and the next sign to Widdop. Cross the footbridge to your right and savour the sound of the moorland stream as it tumbles to the lake. The path runs between a stone drain and the lake proper. On this stretch you are quite close to the water. In early summer there will be clusters of ducks, herding their ducklings to safety, and alarm calls of other birds among the rocks. It is good to watch wild ducks and geese landing on the water.

The trees along this stretch look as if they have had a struggle to survive the winter winds but the air is getting cleaner and many trees now have a much better chance of growth. Beyond Widdop Lodge, cross the bridge on the left to the gate by the road. From here your car is just 200 yards to your left.

Walk No 3

Crimsworth Dean.

Distance 4 miles. Walking time 2 hours.

Refreshments: In summer there is a kiosk in Hardcastle Crags car park.

Start point: Hardcastle Crags car park, Hebden Bridge. Map Reference SD 989291, marked New Bridge, on the South Pennine Leisure Map.

Approaches to the start. Take the A646 along the Calder Valley to Hebden Bridge and then take the road signed to Keighley and Hardcastle Crags. About half a mile up this road bear left down to Midgehole and Hardcastle Crags. There is a National Trust Car Park at the end.

There are miles of paths in Hardcastle Crags that can absorb a huge number of visitors. This walk follows a less used route up Crimsworth Dean. From the car park walk back out of the entrance, crossing the river which provided so much water power for local mills in the past. Take the Calderdale Way track up to your left. Some 60 yards up you come to a junction of four paths which is called Lane Ends. Take the upper left track, signed Bridleway to Pecket Well. Look out for a small gate on the left 80 yards up from Lane Ends, where the Bridleway turns sharp right.

Go through this gate and follow the grass depression across an old green road and then upwards through a sparse wood and across an open field. As the path reaches the far wall it climbs to the stile in the corner into Middle Dean Wood. Pause for breath and admire the view. Your return road is clearly seen across the valley, with Hardcastle Crags behind and Mount Zion Chapel at Slack perched on the skyline behind.

On entering the wood, turn left and continue on more or less the same level, avoiding the path which climbs, soon meeting another path which comes up from the mill ponds below. Continue ahead aided by yellow waymarkers. Middle Dean Wood is lovely in spring with masses of bluebells and wild garlic. The old dams below, which stored water to power water wheels, are interesting but quite dangerous to children. The aqueducts feeding them remind one of the levada walks on the island of Madeira.

Towards the end of the path through the wood the path climbs and, as the trees thin out, you can see a house ahead directly across two fields. This is called Wheat Ing. An Ing is an old Yorkshire word for a field, so wheat would have been grown in this sheltered spot at one time. As you cross the two fields notice the cottage above and behind Wheat Ing, on the opposite side of the valley. This is Outwood Cottage and it is on your route ahead.

At the middle stile, before Wheat Ing, there is a drainage problem where a plank bridge would be useful, if you keep close to the wall you can keep your feet dry.

As soon as you have gone through the gate at Wheat Ing, turn left and follow the path between the post and wire fence and the Hawthorn hedge. You soon see the old causey stones down to Wheat Ing bridge, a delightful spot. Over the bridge climb the steps to the right through Abel Cote Wood. Abel Cote is the name of a farm way above you on the edge of the moors, next to two ancient crosses standing like the brothers Cain and Abel.

As you leave Abel Cote Wood follow the path upwards to join the track that runs down to Outwood Cottage. Turn right along this track to pick up the path which runs behind Outwood Cottage. This is a beautiful valley, still dotted with ruins of Pennine Farms which can no longer make a living out of agriculture. These farms are often in gorgeous locations and if you can afford the cost of improving access and restoration they make wonderful homes. It is a shame to see the state of some dry stone walls, but now we have a Calderdale Dry Stone Walling Association, with master craftsmen and women ready to work, there is hope that our walls will be rebuilt.

When the path meets an old green road, turn right down to Lumb Hole. The waterfalls and the thin arch of Lumb Bridge make a fine sight at any time of year but in the spring, when the banks have a show of marsh marigolds it is particularly pleasant. Lumb Hole is a place which often echos to the sound of children, young and old, enjoying themselves.

Cross Lumb Bridge and follow the bridleway, first to the right then uphill, until you reach Haworth Old Road. Turn right, and after the first farm take the second of two drives on your right. As the drive turns left there is a stile on the left which avoids the farm yard and the dogs at Barker Cote.

The path continues on the same level connecting a line of farms which were built on the spring line, where clear water emerge from below the moors above. You will see causey stones occasionally. Keep the wall on your left, passing below the next farm, Upper Small Shaw, cross the next field to a stile. Once through the stile turn sharp right and follow the wall downhill for one field. At the next field the path goes diagonally left dropping towards the beech wood.

Through the wood take the road down to Wheat Ing, cross the packhorse bridge again and this time turn left over the bridge. The broad track through Abel Cote Wood reveals some good woodland management with plenty of replanting where there is enough light, with the new trees being sheltered by the more mature ones around.

At the gate at the end of the wood the road rises through a field which

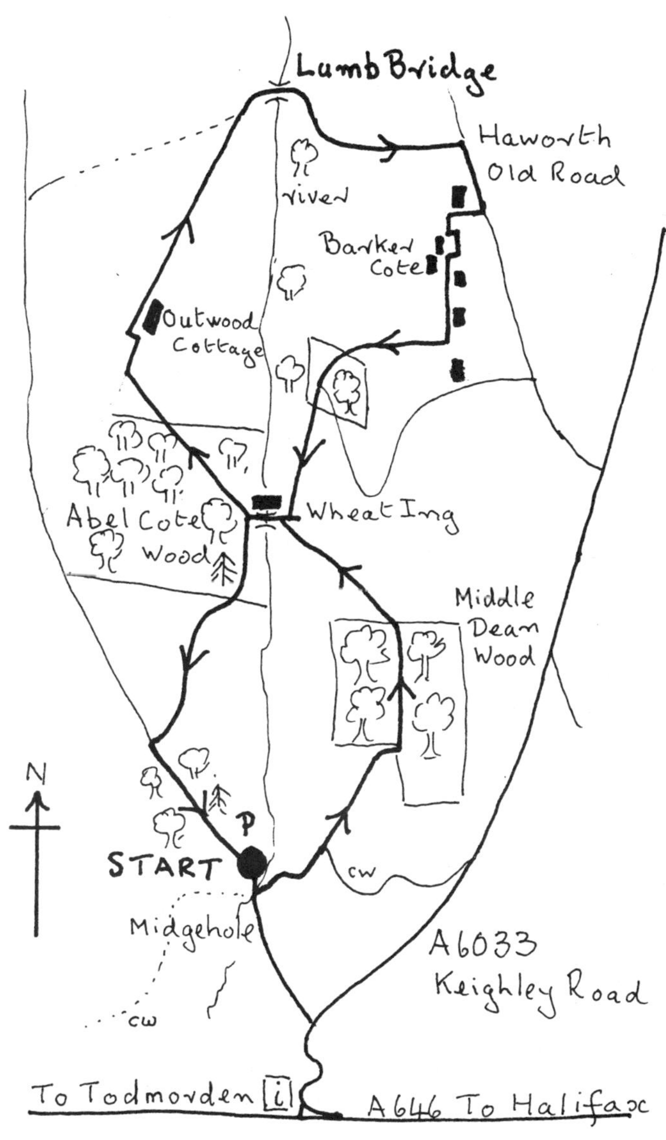

Lumb Bridge
Haworth Old Road
river
Barker Cote
Outwood Cottage
Abel Cote Wood
Wheat Ing
Middle Dean Wood
N
P
START
cw
Midgehole
A6033 Keighley Road
cw
To Todmorden
i
A646 To Halifax

reminds one of an Alpine meadow, full of wild flowers in the spring and the sweet smell of meadow grass, known to chemists as coumarin. At the top gate turn left along the unmade road. There are a couple of strategically placed seats to rest a while and enjoy the scenery before you follow the road down to your starting point.

Walk No 4

Hudson Clough.

Distance 2-3 miles. Walking time 90 minutes.
Refreshments: The Staff of Life, 550 Burnley Road.

Start point: The bottom of Knotts Road, adjacent to 522, Burnley Road, on the A646 from Todmorden to Burnley. Map Reference SD 917286, marked Knotts Wood, on the South Pennine Leisure Map.

At the start of this walk, pause and have a good look around. You are in a deep gorge which the river has cut from the surrounding land since the last ice age. The river has a large catchment area and the power of the water here can be immense. In days gone by this was used to drive many a water wheel.

Above the start point, on the opposite side of the valley is a rocky outcrop known as Eagle Crag, although you can't see the shape of the eagle's head very clearly from here. Sheep cling to the steep hillside and an old packhorse track climbs to the right. The passing motorist feels confined by the valley and you have to take to the hills to see what a wonderful area this is.

Walk up Knotts Road a little way, notice the flexible bridge and the railway embankment. The hillside is on the move. Below on the right you can see Fiddlers Bridge at the start of two old routes. Follow the road upwards until, 50 paces after the tarmac ends, the road doubles back up a grassy track to a little gate onto the open hillside. You are still on Knotts Road, used by horse and cart to bring milk down from Hartley Royd Farm until a landslip blocked the road in 1947. Don't be tempted to take a short cut up the hillside, keep to the track.

As you round the first bend on the open hillside you can see the remains of Roundfield Farm on the skyline opposite. This is south facing, it has not been renovated and yet access from above would not be too difficult once a drainage problem has been solved. Around the second bend the hamlet of Shore comes into view with its lovely old Baptist Chapel. This is another listed building but the roof has collapsed. Restoration here would provide more than one house. As you reach a clump of oak trees, where a landslip has occurred, the route we want doubles back uphill to the right. It is a steady climb which gives a good perspective over the country town of Todmorden.

Todmorden is a great place to live and work. It is large enough to have a thriving community life with over 200 clubs, societies and associations, and yet its fast rail links make its relative isolation easily accessible to all stations between Manchester and Leeds. The houses are clustered together at the junction of three valleys and above the town the agricultural plain gradually rises to the wild open Yorkshire Moors.

The peace monument on Stoodley Pike is soon seen, with Whirlaw Stones on the near left and Great Bride Stones behind. The rocks just across the valley, called Orchan Rocks, are on the return route. Below the wood under Orchan Rocks you can see the remains of Jumps Mill where the old roof at this end has been replaced by a flat roof. This still contains a water wheel built between two walls.

The track doubles back to the left where the wall meets an upper wall at a stone end-post. Towards the top of Knotts Road there is a steep drop on the right some 200 feet down to the river. Keep well away from the edge, especially if it is windy! The track curves into the hill, passing a radio mast, and on to Hartley Royd. At the time of writing some of its windows are still blocked from the days of the window tax but the time can not be far distant when restoration will bring the whole of this fine house back into use. Look out for date stones as you pass through the yard.

Once through the yard, take the path through the little gate ahead into the field and after 40 yards turn right down to Hudson Bridge. There is a line of causey stones here which are sometimes covered in grass and at other times covered in water. You can keep dry by walking on the high side.

Hudson Bridge is the best preserved packhorse bridge in Todmorden. There is a report that it connects to a Roman Road which then crosses Hudson Moor. Indeed, some students from the Lancashire Polytechnic at Preston excavated it some years ago. When it had been measured and photographed it was re-covered for posterity. The word Roman is often used in this locality to describe anything old. The 'Roman' barrow turned out to be middle bronze age, about 1500 BC and the 'Roman' road at Blackstone Edge probably only dates from the wars of the Roses.

From Hudson Bridge take the path to the right across Hudson Moor passing various old quarries. As you meet the far wall you come to a little gate on the right. Continue downhill, below Orchan Rocks, towards the wood. When you meet Jumps Lane turn right and continue downhill. On your right you get good views of Robinwood Mill, with the line of Workers Houses to the left on Robinwood Terrace, and the manager's house overlooking them all behind on the hillside. The lane descends through Kitson Wood, full of mature beech trees that make a fine sight in spring and autumn.

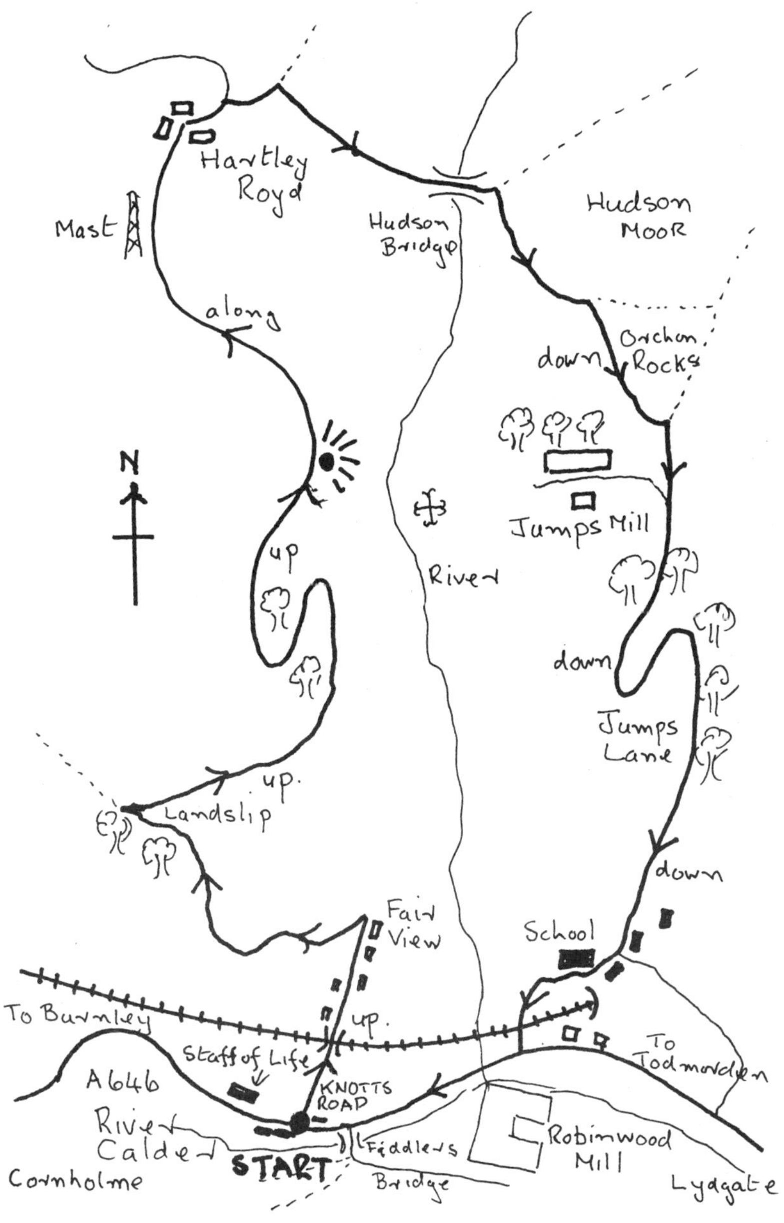

Hartley Royd
Mast
Hudson Bridge
Hudson MOOR
along
Orchan Rocks
down
N
Jumps Mill
up
River
down
Jumps Lane
up.
Landslip
down
Fair View
School
To Burnley
up.
Staff of Life
To Todmorden
A646
KNOTTS ROAD
River Calder
Fiddlers Bridge
Robinwood Mill
START
Cornholme
Lydgate

When you reach the first houses keep right, passing Robinwood School and going twice through the arches of the viaduct to the main road. A short walk to the right will bring you back to the start. As you go, study the land at the side of Robinwood Mill and see if you can pick out the site of the old pond and aqueduct which fed a huge overshot water wheel on the back of the mill. The water intake is just above Fiddlers Bridge. Robinwood Mill was built by William Fairburn in about 1835. It once faced demolition, but now the new owner is to undertake restoration.

Walk No 5

Heptonstall's Natural Defences.

Distance 2-3 miles. Walking time 90 minutes.

Refreshments: The Cross Inn or The White Lion, Heptonstall.

Start point: Car park in the centre of Heptonstall village. Map Reference SD 988282 on the South Pennine Leisure Map. Heptonstall is a hill village and to reach it from the valley bottom, on the Hebden Bridge to Todmorden Road (A646), traffic from Hebden Bridge has to use the turning circle.

Leave the car park by the route you entered and walk uphill towards the church. Take the old lane on the left, which is signed to the Museum, even though it is called Church Lane. Follow it round to the left, walking between the Church and West Laith, bearing left at the end until you turn at the Calderdale Way sign on the right. Leaving the trees behind follow the wall on the left down Eaves Lane.

As you go, the peace monument on Stoodley Pike stands proud with Horschold below it in the foreground. Horsehold has a long association with horses, stretching from the days of Erringden Deer Park to the days of horse drawn canal bages. At the end of their work, the horses would leave the canal and climb the long cobbled road to the stables and meadows above.

When you reach the edge of the valley a spectacular view opens up. This is the south wall of Heptonstall's natural defences. By all means peer over the edge and look at the top of Hell Hole but don't explore too far as our route lies to the right, along the wall side, above Eaves Wood. Keep to the top path as you go.

The house beyond the wood, half way up the hillside is called Lumb Bank. Once the home of Ted Hughes, our Poet Laureate, it is now occupied by the Arvon Foundation and is used as a resource to encourage writers. Lumb is an old word for chimney. All the valleys round here once had water powered mills. When the steam engine was invented they switched to steam power and a hundred years ago the valley was filled with chimneys belching smoke. If the chimney was in the valley bottom, it did not get much wind and so the Lumbs were built up the hill side. Hence the name Lumb Bank. Several chimneys remain in apparent isolation.

The path along the top of Eaves Wood gets into a bit of a scramble over gritstone boulders but you soon reach the road to Lumb Bank. Turn downhill for 100 yards to the first bend where you take the level track on the right. Once past Lumb Bank the track climbs to a junction of five paths. The one we want is the broad green track going up to the right to Popples Common. The surrounding meadows are a mass of wild flowers in the spring.

When you have passed the new houses at Popples Common, with the old Chapel and Sunday School half right, turn right down to Slack Top. When you reach the road, go down for 70 yards and take the path signed to Hardcastle Crags, next to number 30. The deep wooded valley of Hardcastle Crags curves away to the left and Crimsworth Dean to the right. Above them, in a typical Pennine landscape, the farms use the agricultural plain until the tree-less moors take over. It is obvious that trees can grow round here, and that they have been cleared for agriculture. Thankfully now there is a greater awareness of the value of trees and much replanting is being done.

When you reach the tree line, turn right and take the path which keeps above the wood. Below you is the Scout Hostel and you may be regaled with the smell of woodsmoke and outdoor cooking. Where the path divides take the higher one along the top of the wall. Now you are inspecting the north flank of Heptonstall's defences and, if you happen to be here in late July, there will be plenty of bilberries around.

Eventually you climb some steps to a meadow path to the road. The meadow is the site of Dawson City, the southern terminus of the Blake Dean railway. This was built in 1900 for the constuction of the Walshaw Dean Reservoirs. At its peak, 15 steam engines were employed. The engines had a three foot gauge and were delivered to Hebden Bridge railway station. They then had to be hauled up to Dawson City by a team of 21 heavy horses! This had to wait until a saturday afternoon when most of the horses were free from normal duties. It's hard to imagine that this meadow was once a busy railway yard. Walk 17 goes along more of the route of Blake Dean railway.

When you cross the road the field path continues 50 yards to the left. As you cross the next meadow all the best views are behind you. It is worth a pause to look up the length of Crimsworth Dean (Walk No.3). At the next stile bear left to pick up the walled lane which eventually becomes Townfield Lane. As you go, Hebden Bridge is gradually revealed below.

When you reach Weavers Square in the village, refreshments are to hand in the White Lion and Cross Inn below you. It is worth a visit to The Paper Shop to pick up a copy of the Heptonstall Trail booklet, and some fine postcards by Peter Hollins, to remind you of your visit to this historic village.

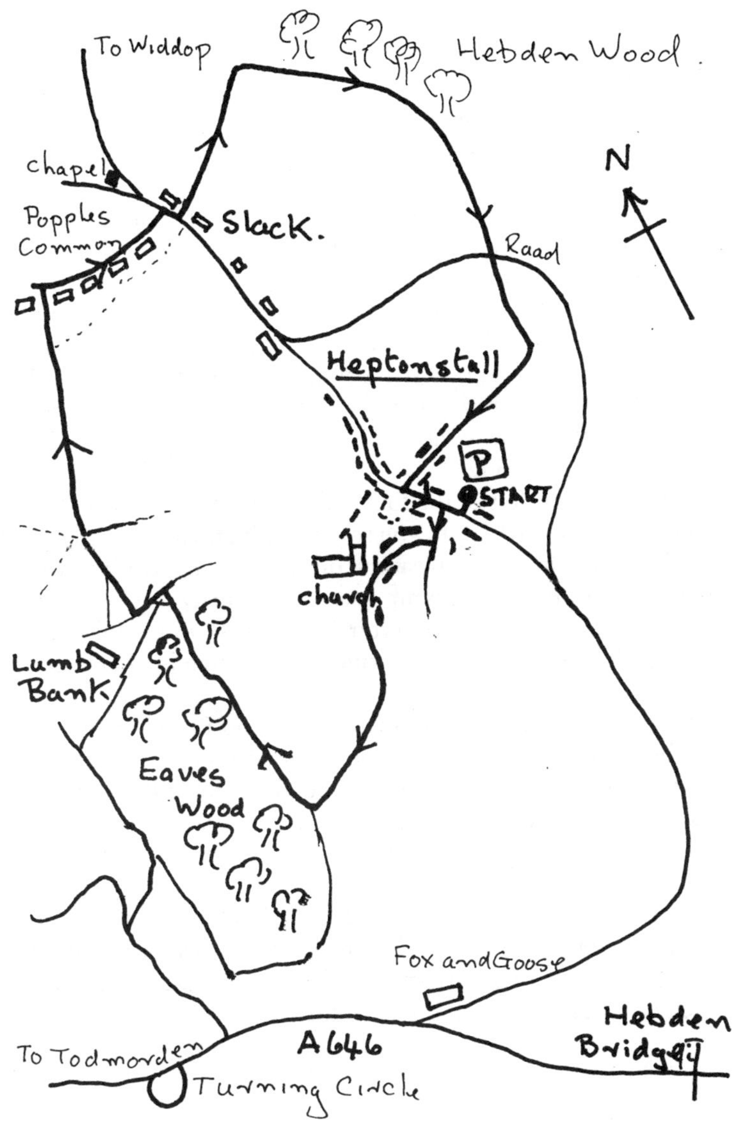
To Widdop
Hebden Wood
N
chapel
Popples Common
Slack.
Road
Heptonstall
P
START
church
Lumb Bank
Eaves Wood
Fox and Goose
Hebden Bridge
A646
To Todmorden
Turning Circle

Walk No 6
Hurstwood.

Distance 2 miles. Walking time 1 hour.
Refreshments: The Kettledrum at Mereclough or go to Worsthorne.

Start point: Car park at Hurstwood, Map reference: SD 882313.

Leave the car park by the route you entered, cross the bridge over the river Brun and admire the enormous barn opposite. Turn right, walking past the former Chapel and lovely old cottages. As the road curves into the farmyard at the end, take the way-marked stile ahead. The path immediatly climbs to skirt the top side of the wood. When you have been walking above the wood for a few minutes, look out for a stile on your right which takes you through the wood to the reservoir. Follow this path to the far side but don't cross the footbridge.

Take the path to the left of the footbridge, which skirts the lower side of the wood for a few yards, until you see the path down to the edge of the reservoir. This stretch is very pleasant on a summer morning, when it becomes a real suntrap. The trees are reaching maturity nicely. They were planted in 1927 to screen the reservoir from Hurstwood Village. Walk along to the little wood at the end, taking the right hand path close to the reservoir.

You soon leave the trees and follow Hurstwood Brook upstream to a crossing. The walk now follows the opposite bank along the reservoir back to the start point. You must have wondered about the hillocky nature of the landscape. In this area the land has been dug for stone, coal, limestone, and even lead ores, but the majority of the old workings around Hurstwood were for stone.

When you reach the tree-lined road, the right of way does not go through the gate, but takes the road to the left for a yard or two until you can turn right, through a kissing gate and a few trees, to the road. From here it is but ten minutes walk back down to the car park.

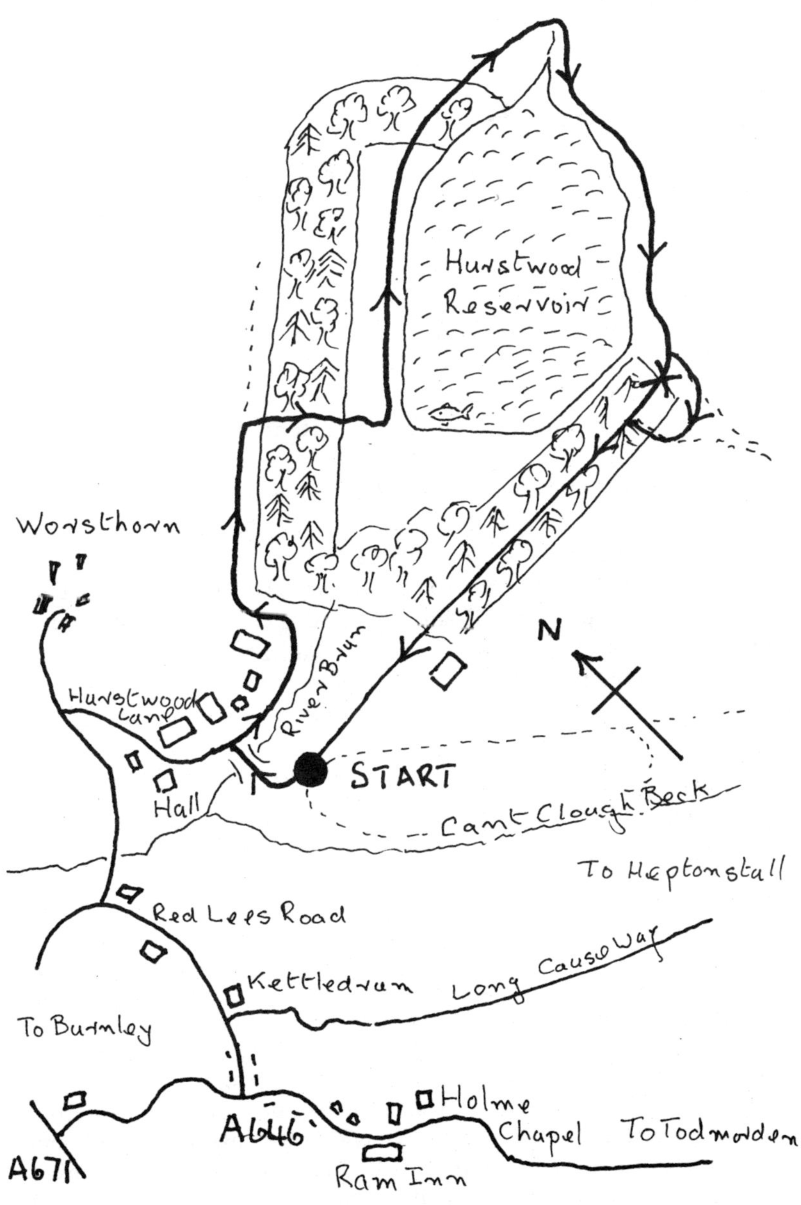
Hurstwood Reservoir
Worsthorn
N
River Brun
Hurstwood Lane
START
Hall
Cant Clough Beck
To Heptonstall
Red Lees Road
Kettledrum
Long Causeway
To Burnley
Holme
Chapel
To Todmorden
A646
A671
Ram Inn

Walk No 7

Shedden Clough.

Distance 1.5 miles. Walking time: allow 1 hour.
Refreshments: The Sportsmans Arms at Kebcote, south of the start or the Kettledrum at Mereclough, north of the start.

Start point: Car park on the Long Causeway, Map reference: SD 894288 on the South Pennine Leisure Map.

The start is best reached from the A646 Burnley to Halifax Road. The turn-off depends where you are coming from. From Burnley leave the A646 at Cliviger, turning left into Red Lees Road, then turn right at the Kettledrum Pub.

From Todmorden, follow the A646 Halifax Road for 1/2 a mile, turning left up Cross Stone Road and left again at the next three junctions. The car park is 2.8 miles beyond the Sportsman's Arms.

From Halifax follow the A646 to Hebden Bridge. After two sets of lights take the first right up Church Road. The road is very steep and winding, giving magnificent views across to Heptonstall and the Calder Valley. Once you are on the top the route is straight ahead for 5 miles passing the Shoulder of Mutton at Blackshaw Head and the Sportsman's Arms at Kebcote.

The car park has been made by the North West Water Authority and is quite remote, so please make sure that you car is locked and secure before you leave it.

You may like to see the carving on a gatepost on the opposite side of the road which says Maiden Cross. This is certainly not the original cross but close to the original site. Joshua Holden in his "Shorter History of Todmorden" (1912) recounts that Maiden Cross is the place where one of Charles Townley's men said goodbye to his sweetheart before going off to fight in the days of the Cavaliers and Roundheads. He never returned and the woman frantic in her grief resorted to this cross where she had last seen her lover.

The road itself was once a long line of causey stones. A very ancient route, present long before the Romans came. Titus Thornber, in his book "A Pennine Parish, a history of Cliviger" lists some of the Roman coins found along the Long Causeway. There are two bronze age burial grounds, about 3500 years old, just off the Causeway, but that's another story.

The Shedden Valley contains old limestone hushings which are quite fascinating. Although they have been known for centuries it was Titus

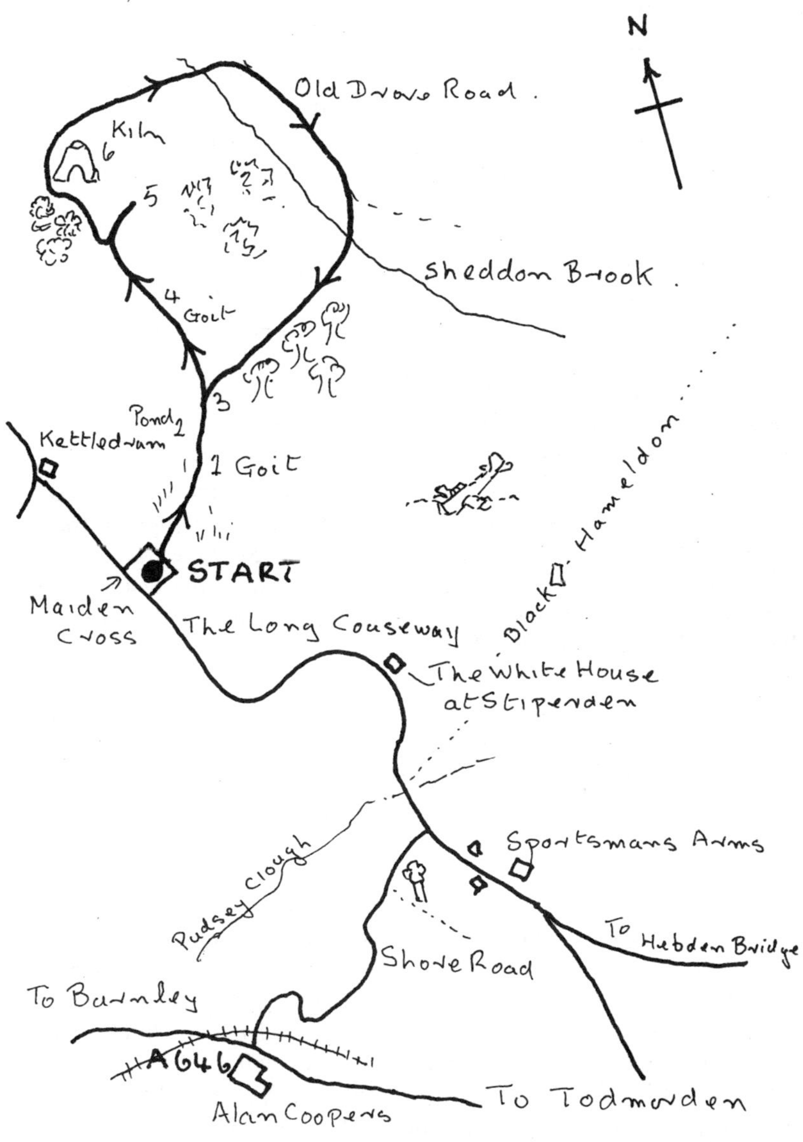

N
Old Drove Road
Kiln
6
5
Sheddon Brook
4
Goit
3
Pond 2
Kettledram
1 Goit
START
Black Hameldon
Maiden Cross
The Long Couseway
The White House at Stipenden
Sportsmans Arms
Pudsey Clough
To Hebden Bridge
Shore Road
To Burnley
A646
Alan Coopers
To Todmorden

Thornber, of Middle Pasture Farm, who brought them to the attention of the present generation. I was lucky enough to hear him speak to the Todmorden Antiquarian Society and became keen to inspect them for myself. Fortunately Titus has raised so much interest in the area that the North West Water Board, who own the land, and Burnley Council have used the Community Programme to make them more accessible to the public. They would make an interesting half-day excursion for a school party with perhaps a visit to Townley Hall or Queen Street Mill for the other half.

The story starts with the last ice age about 12,000 years ago. We know that the South Pennines have been covered by glaciers at least three times but, on the last occasion, the glacier stopped at Black Hameldon. The ice moving from the north deposited most of its moraine debris from the north in Shedden and Hurstwood. It is quite usual to find rocks and limestone from much farther north in the stream bed. This limestone was used to sweeten the land and to make mortar when the timber frame houses were being replaced with stone houses from about the year 1450.

The problem of how to find the lumps of limestone was solved by hushing. Water would be brought by goits (ditches) from high up the hill to large storage ponds. When the pond was full, the whole contents were suddenly discharged by breaching a wall. This caused the water to rush downhill, washing away the top soil to reveal the stones. The limestone was collected and burnt in lime kilns and the other stone was thrown onto spoil heaps.

So, on this walk you need to look for:

1. long goits or ditches coming down from the uplands,
2. the site of holding ponds,
3. the deep v-shaped hushings below the ponds,
4. the pile of unwanted stone and
5. the lime kilns.

Some of the goits can be followed for more than a mile and there are over a hundred old kilns in the area. Walk through the wooden kissing gate and follow the path downhill for a few minutes until you come to a wooden post marked 1. This is the first of seven posts signing things of interest. Post number 1 marks a main inlet goit coming down from the hills. At post number 2 you can see the site of a pond on your left.

At post number 3 go straight ahead, do not follow the old drove road coming up from the right. You are now following another inlet goit. Go through the next stile, keeping to the line of the goit which soon feeds into a pond site marked with a yellow circle. At post 4 look right beyond the drove road to two trees standing on a hummocky ridge. There is another pond marker on top of the hummock to the left of the trees. All the land between has been washed away by hushing!

The trail crosses an outlet goit which could have taken water to another pond to post 5, which appears to be a general viewpoint. Looking back you can see the deep v-shaped hushings and the piles of unwanted stones thrown to one side. Retrace your steps to the path on the right which descends through the rhodedendron bushes. These have been introduced relativly recently and could spread for miles, as they have in Wales.

As you emerge from the bushes, into an area littered with stone piles, follow the path to a re-built kiln at post number 6. Many of them where built so that the hollow on one side would catch the prevailing wind to blow the fire. The fuel could have been wood but coal is still available within half a mile at Merrill Head. I think limestone (calcium carbonate) and coal would be tipped in at the top and the quicklime (calcium oxide) and coal ash dug out at the bottom. If water was added to this mixture you would get lime (calcium hydroxide).

The path beyond the kiln winds down to the right to join the old drove road at post number 7. At this point turn right and go up the road. Much of the dry stone walling has been very well re-built under the Community Programme. Goodness knows how the work will be completed when this programme comes to an end.

As you go up the drove road there is a gate on your left which leads to a part of the hushings that have not been restored. Should you decide to do a little exploration for yourself take care and don't disturb other sites yet to be researched. The tops of kilns are recognised by greener grass and plants which enjoy the lime-rich environment. The white moraine limestone is still to be found along the tributaries of Shedden Brook. The drovers road returns to post number 3, from whence you can retrace your route back to the car.

Walk No 8
Stoodley Pike.

Distance 3 miles. Walking time: 1-2 hours.
Refreshments: The Top Brink at Lumbutts, open from 7pm and at lunch time each weekend.

Start point: The road from Lumbutts to Mankinholes. Map reference: SD 957234 on the South Pennine Leisure Map. There are several places where safe roadside parking can be made close to Lumbutts Chapel. Approching from the south, leave the A6033 Littleborough to Todmorden Road at Walsden Post Office and follow the signs to Lumbutts. Approching from Todmorden, take the A646 Halifax Road for 1 mile, just after you you have passed over the brow of a hill, turn right up Woodhouse Road, where there is a sign Public Footpath to Mankinholes. At the top of the hill, turn left and drive through Lumbutts Village to the chapel on your left.

A Footpath sign opposite Lumbutts Chapel indicates the start of the route to Stoodley Pike. Stoodley Pike is a hill, but the great peace monument on top of the hill has also acquired the name. You start up a broad bridleway and soon become aware of a line of old causey stones which occasionally break the surface. These are part of the network of packhorse routes which predate modern roads. The South Pennines have many such causeways, often still in good condition after hundreds of years use.

At the first gate you reach the open area of Langfield Common. The stone stile next to the gate gives you a resting place to look back. The two dams, below you and to the left, fed three water wheels, one below the other in the tower of Lumbutts Mill. Together they generated 54 horse power. The tower is still there, together with its spiral staircase, but the mill and the wheels have gone. To your right the old hamlet of Mankinholes remains even though many a barn has been refurbished to make very pleasant houses.

Continue up the Long Causeway, at a very steady pace, if you attempt to go too quickly you will soon have to pause for breath.

Below you is Stansfield View, once a workhouse, now a hospital. The idea of a workhouse, set up by the poor law, was an anathema to John Fielden. He was both a partner in Fielden Brothers, who owned many mills in Todmorden, and MP for Oldham from 1832 to 1847. He fiercly resisted the implementation of the poor law. His pamphlet "The curse of the factory system" makes clear his view that many workers were not

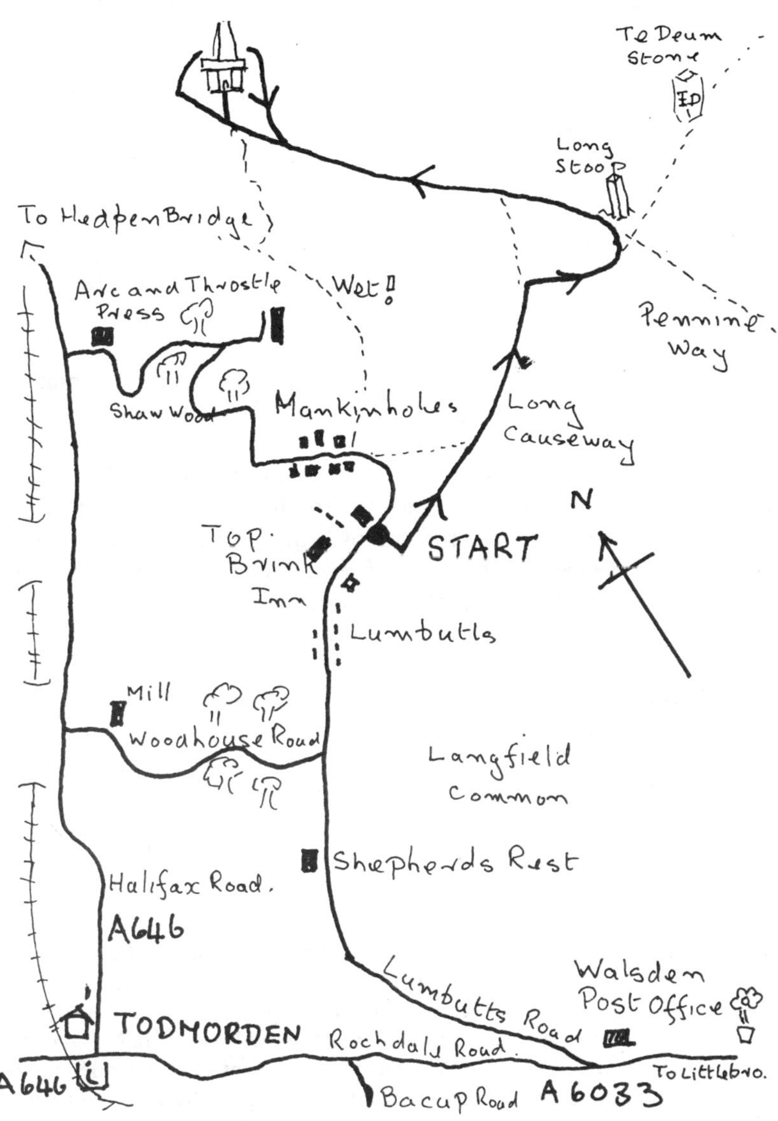

Te Deum Stone
Long Stoop
To Hedpen Bridge
Arc and Throstle Press
Wet!
Pennine Way
Shaw Wood
Mankinholes
Long Causeway
N
Top Brink Inn
START
Lumbutts
Mill
Woodhouse Road
Langfield Common
Shepherds Rest
Halifax Road.
A646
Lumbutts Road
Walsden Post Office
TODMORDEN
Rochdale Road.
A646
To Littlebro.
Bacup Road
A6033

responsible for their own poverty. Consequently Todmorden's workhouse was not built until long after his death and when it was, the quality of building was so good that it could make a fine hotel when the hospital closes.

As the causeway approaches the top it takes a right turn, follow it up and notice the seat up to the left in memory of Arthur Archer, one time warden of Mankinholes Youth Hostel. The view from this seat is tremendous. In the distant valley you can see Robinwood Viaduct, and to its left the great structure of Robinwood Mill, built about 1835, with a huge overshot water wheel that could power six floors. To your left you can see the straight line of Withins New Road, that starts from the Shepherd's Rest and climbs steadily to Withins Gate behind you. Withins New Road was built during the cotton famine to convey the Fielden's carriages to their lodge in Cragg Vale.

Behind you is a leaning stone known as Long Stoop. This is a landmark for miles and many local folk like its jaunty angle, but how long it will defy wind and gravity goodness only knows. Long Stoop marks the southern junction of the Pennine Way and the vastly more interesting Calderdale Way. It is worth delaying our journey to Stoodley Pike just to follow the Long Causeway across the top to Withins Gate, because just through the gate we find the Te Deum Stone, one of several stones with Latin in these parts. Te Deum Laudamus means we praise thee o God. I have asked many people who the initials I D refer to but have never found an answer.

From the Te Deum stone you can see the wild surrounds of Withins Clough (Walk No. 21). Once the home of bronze age man, it even held 17 farms until the building of the reservoir - part of the price we pay for clean water. From the Te Deum stone it is time to retrace our steps to Long Stoop, and to turn right following the Pennine Way on a twenty minute journey towards the monument on Stoodley Pike. As you go, admire the setting of Todmorden, a country town with good rail links to both sides of the Pennines.

The site on Stoodley Pike was probably used for bronze age burials, since bones were found when excavating for the first circular tower. This was built in 1815 to celebrate the peace at the end of the Napoleonic War. Unfortunately, it collapsed when the next war started, on the day the Russian ambassador left London before the Crimean war. The present monument was built in 1856. You can climb up the inner spiral staircase counting 39 steps in the dark to get a great view.Stoodley Pike may also have been a beacon site. A beacon was temporarily erected and lit on 19th July 1988 to commemorate the great chain of beacons 400 years earlier when the Spanish Armada was sighted of the southern coast.

There are two routes back to your car. You could drop down from the edge of the hill opposite the stair of the monument. This is steep and zig zags. It then follows a wet bridleway to the left back to Mankinholes. Not to be recommended until the drainage of the bridleway is improved. It is better to retrace your steps from Stoodley Pike to Long Stoop and drop down the Long Causeway. The views are still magnificent but different because you are going the other way!

Walk No 9
Wycoller.

Distance 2 miles. Walking time 1 hour.
Refreshments: The Craft Centre Coffee Shop.

Start point: Wycoller Car Park. Map reference: SD 925396 on the South Pennine Leisure Map.

Approach from Burnley. Follow the M65 to Colne, then take the A6068 signed to Keighley. Turn off right, signed to Trawden, about a mile out of Colne. On the way to Trawden turn off left signed to Wycoller. From Calderdale, go to Hebden Bridge then take the Road to Heptonstall and Slack where you take the right fork up the valley beyond Widdop, turning right to Trawden as you drop down into Lancashire. If you get to Trawden and have still not found the turn off to Wycoller, take the road signed to Keighley for a mile, looking out for a right fork.

Although this is perhaps the shortest walk in this book, and most of it is level going, you should allow plenty of time for sightseeing. It needs carefull observation to spot all the fascination of Wycoller. Until fairly recently Wycoller was a deserted hamlet, renowned for the beautiful bridges over the beck and the romantic ruins of Wycoller Hall, reputedly used by Charlotte Bronte as the setting for Ferndale Manor in Jane Eyre.

The hamlet was once occupied by farmers and hand-loom weavers but as power looms moved into Colne the workers moved to where the money was, leaving Wycoller deserted. For a few years a group of dedicated people formed themselves into the Friends of Wycoller and set about re-occupation and restoration. Then Lancashire County Council took a hand and formed the Wycoller Country Park. Now all the houses are occupied, although you can still find old farms without their rooves in the Forest of Trawden this is a success story of conservation and restoration.

The Old Hall still remains as a ruin but its barn is now a Village Information Centre, open at weekends and bank holidays from 10am to 5 pm. Wycoller could be the starting point for many more walks. The Bronte Way goes over the moor to Haworth. The Pendle Way goes off in the other direction. The progressive policy of the North West Water Authority in granting a permissive path up Boulsworth Hill to Lad Law gives us the chance to view the South Pennines from one of its most impressive high peaks.

From Wycoller Car Park follow the footpath for a few minutes to this remote hamlet. Note the standing stones which once formed field wall on

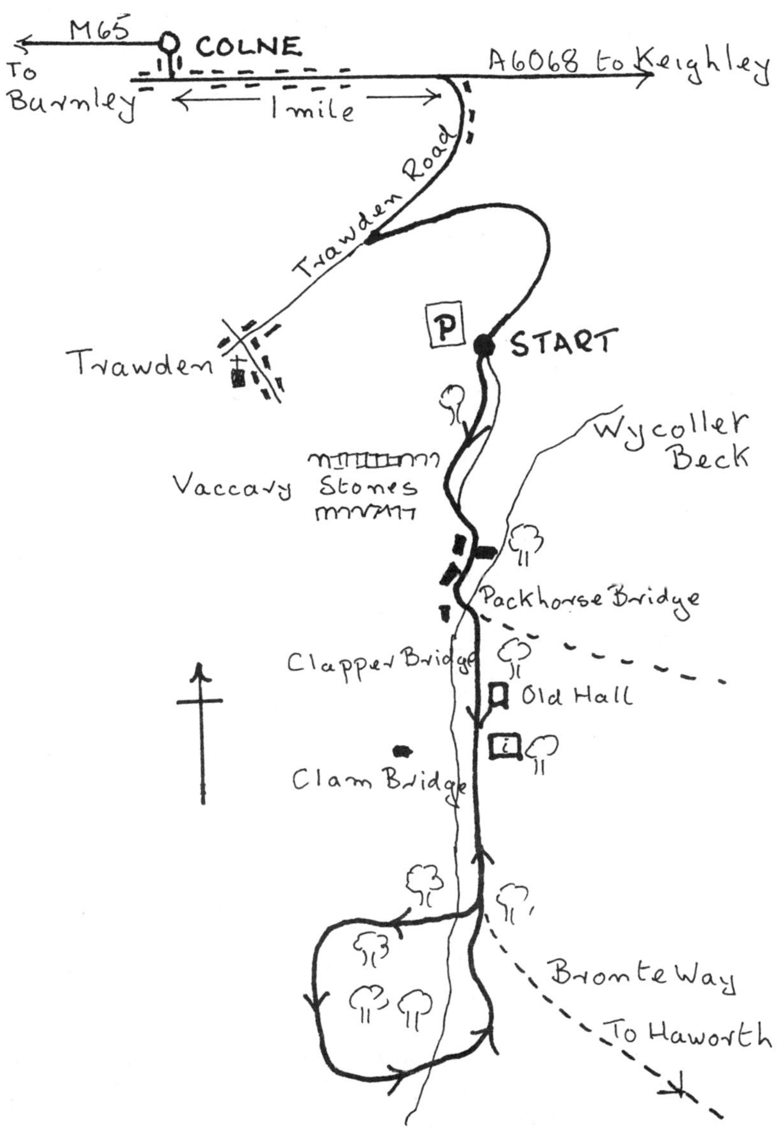
M65
COLNE
To
Burnley
A6068 to Keighley
1 mile
Trawden Road
Trawden
P
START
Wycoller
Beck
Vaccary Stones
Packhorse Bridge
Clapper Bridge
Old Hall
i
Clam Bridge
Bronte Way
To Haworth

your right. These are vaccary stones erected in the fourteenth century by the De Lacy's, Lords of the Manor of Clitheroe. At one time there were no dry stone walls so cattle could interbreed at will. In order to improve the stock good bulls had to be mated with good cows and inferior bulls were kept away. These vaccary walls are the precursors of our more familiar dry stone walls which were built when Parliament passed the enclosure acts, for the same purpose of improving farming stock. Wycoller had two vaccaries.

As you enter the hamlet proper the fine door of Pearsons House on the left gives you the flavour of these lovely old buildings. Note the squint hole in the porch to view visitors before opening! At the left hand end, quite close to the ground, notice the holes in the stone. These are the remains of an early centrifuge. When wool had been spun into thread and wound onto a bobbin, the bobbin was then placed in the stream to bind the fibres together. The wet bobbins were quick-dried by placing them in a basket threaded into a stick. One end of the stick was placed in a depression in the wall and the other end was moved quickly with a circular motion (wuzzing is the local word) throwing the water out.

Perhaps the next things which strike your eye are the two bridges, the ford and the ruins of the hall beyond. The first bridge is an old packhorse bridge, built about 1400, with its causey stones worn by generations of clog irons and horse shoes. The other bridge is a three stone clapper bridge with the horizontal stones mounted on verticals in the stream. The arched bridges that we know today were introduced into England by the Romans. To build a clapper bridge you had to know how to move large blocks of stone.

Explore the hall and the Information Centre if it is open. Beyond the information Centre, is what appears to be a duck pond with plenty of ducks and ducklings. This was an ornamental pond for the Cunliffe family who lived in the hall. Today picnic tables allow everyone to enjoy the pond. Above the pond is a cockpit used for cock fights. Stanley Cookson and Herbert Hindle, in their book "Wycoller" recount that we get our name for a cocktail from the toast that was drunk to the winning cock. The number of tail feathers left in the winner determined the number of ingredients in the cocktail.

Follow the track along the side of Wycoller Beck to the amazing clam bridge made of a single stone spanning the beck, this is the oldest type of bridge known to man. The single stone must weigh well over a tonne. Fifty yards beyond the clam bridge we come to a six arm sign post and behind it is a stile. This is a signed short circular walk along the side of the beck. Follow the route to the first footbridge keeping your eye open for squirrels. Over the bridge turn left to the next bridge and return to the six armed sign post on the opposite bank of the beck and then back into the village. It is worth popping into the Craft Centre Coffee Shop where an iron victorian range warms visitors in the winter.

Walk No 10

Trawden and Lad Law.

Distance 5 miles. Walking time: 3 hours.

Start point: Trawden Village. Map reference: SD 915381 marked Hollin Hall on the South Pennine Leisure Map.

Approach from Burnley. Follow the M65 to Colne, then take the A6068 signed to Keighley. Turn off right, signed to Trawden, about a mile out of Colne. From Calderdale, go to Hebden Bridge then take the Road to Heptonstall and Slack where you take the right fork up the valley beyond Widdop, turning right to Trawden as you drop down into Lancashire. The road to Hollin Hall is a cul-de sac and parking space is limited. It is best to drive along to the mill, looking for parking, and then to turn around and drive back to a space where you will not inconvenience anyone.

Trawden is the nearest access point to Boulsworth Hill and the prominent stones on top known as Lad Law. From many points in the South Pennines Lad Law stands above all other hills - high, remote, and romantic. For many years this has been private land but now the North West Water Authority have opened up a concessionary route to Lad Law and we can all enjoy one of the greatest panoramic views in the South Pennines. I had some doubts about including the walk to Lad law in this book because it is not an easy climb. The final pull up to Lad Law is a wet slog, but well worth it. If you feel that the final climb is too much it can be easily left out.

When you have parked your car, walk back towards the mill. The long back of Boulsworth Hill is in front of you and for the first part we go for an easy climb to the right. Turn right, before the mill, at the road narrows sign, up the track to Slack Laithe Farm. As you approach the farm you can see the path ahead through a stile on the hill to the left. As you enter the farmyard, turn sharp left. The first stile is behind the shed on your right. Then climb diagonally left.

You soon gain height and can see across the Forest of Trawden, once hunted for deer and wild boar, now relativly treeless. Bear left after the next stile and make for an old track which runs above the wall to farms, marked on the map as Naze End, Oaken Bank and Antley Gate. When you approach a white cottage, there seems to be a blockage across the track, but a small gate has been provided for you on the right of way. Pass behind the next house and continue towards the cluster of buildings at Oaken Bank. As you approach the farm yard take the right track up behind Alder Hurst

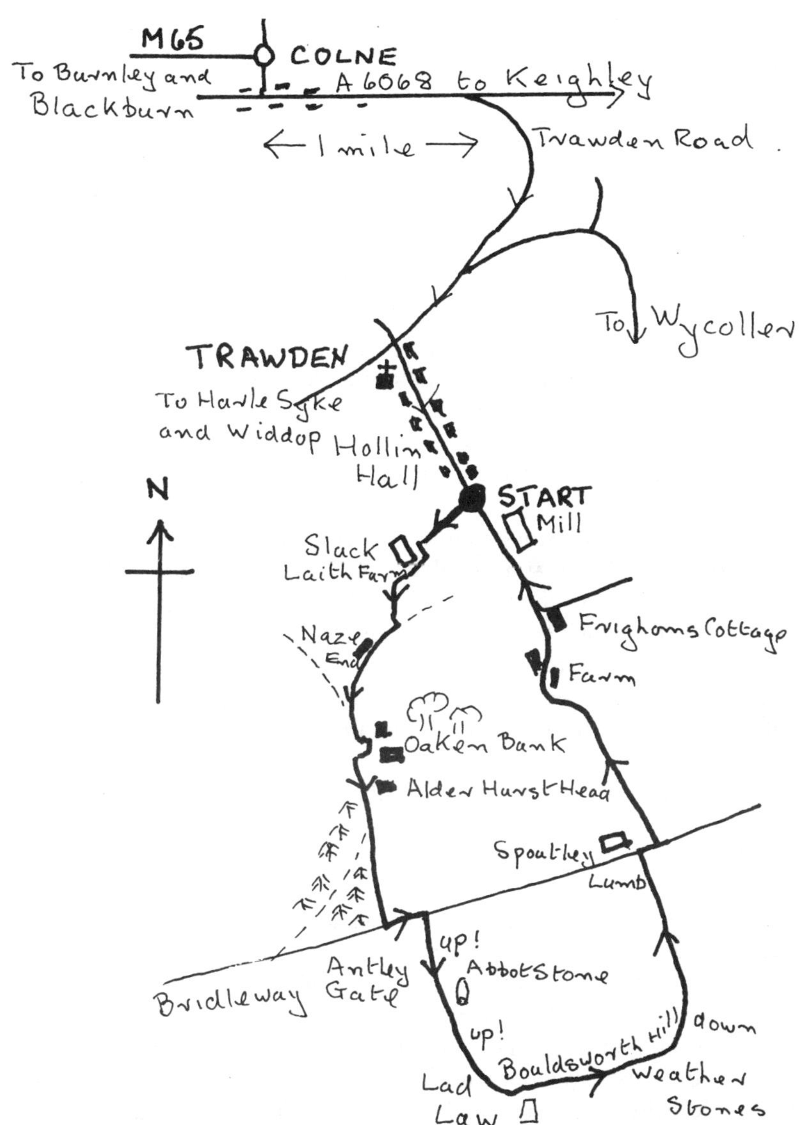
M65
COLNE
To Burnley and Blackburn
A6068 to Keighley
1 mile
Trawden Road
To Wycoller
TRAWDEN
To Harle Syke and Widdop
Hollin Hall
N
START
Mill
Slack Laith Farm
Frighams Cottage
Naze End
Farm
Oaken Bank
Alder Hurst Head
Spoutley Lumb
up!
Abbot Stone
Antley Gate
Bridleway
up!
down
Bouldsworth Hill
Lad Law
Weather Stones

Head Farm. This is sheep country, do be careful to close gates and keep dogs on a lead. You may see Jacob sheep with black spots rather like Dalmatian dogs.

After Alder Hurst Head, the paths divide. We want the one which appears to be a sunken rush-filled road that follows the wall on the left. The field to the right has been planted with christmas trees. Make your way between the trees and the wall. The last 100 yards to the next stile is wet. Continue along the line of the post and wire fence to the ruins at Antley Gate. Ahead lies Boulsworth Hill. The route up to a rock that looks like a bishops mitre, Abbot Stone, is clearly seen. It starts off following the line of a wall up the hill.

To reach the start of the permissive path, go through Antley Gate onto the open moor and take the track to the left across a ford. The start point is well marked with an engraved map provided by the water authority - well done! If the climb looks too daunting you can omit it and continue along the track to where the concessionary route comes down again. This is over to your left where a power line appears to stop in the middle of nowhere. In fact it takes power to an underground reservoir above Spoutly Lumb.

To get up to Abbot Stone follow the path and seven waymarker posts. Have a rest at each one and look back. As you climb distant hills appear. At first you can see Ingleborough with its flat top. to the right is Pen-y-Gent and to the left the long back of Whernside. Pendle Hill, of the Lancashire Witches fame, dominates the left foreground. Once you reach Abbot Stone there are three more waymarkers to the triangulation point on the top.

If you thought the view of Pendle and the Forest of Trawden was stunning on the way up, the view to the south from the summit is spectacular. The South Pennines are laid out in rows in front of you. In the foreground, the rarely seen Dove Stones glisten after a shower, beyond them Widdop Valley, with Gorple Cottages just popping out, backed by Heptonstall Moor. Beyond that we look down far below, to the peace monument on Stoodley Pike above the Calder Valley, and to two ranges of hills beyond. In the foreground the light green road went to a drilling rig which was used for oil exploration in the 1960's.

To the south west Black Hameldon straddles the boundary between Calderdale and Burnley. Dr Whittaker, in his book "The History of Whalley" describes how the same boundary at Wolf Stones, going back in time, marked divisions between the Counties of Yorkshire and Lancashire, the Diocese of York Lichfield, the Provinces of York and Canterbury, and the Kingdoms Mercia and Strathclyde. In the distant west you can see the TV transmitter on windy hill above Bolton. Looking to the north west on a clear day you can see Blackpool Tower and the Lakeland Hills. To the south east the summit of Cockhill (on the road from Keighley to Hebden Bridge) hides Halifax.

> Lad Law stone is about 100 yards west of the summit. The shapes of these gritstones, weathered by wind and water, gives rise to many a Legend. Some say the Druids met here. There are certainly lots of bronze age burial sites in the South Pennines - many have been excavated by archeologists. In Townley Hall Museum there is an earthenware beaker, dated about 2500 BC, which was used as a beer mug by the earlier "beaker" people. This is the oldest beer mug in Lancashire!

From the summit, follow the marker posts to the east past Weather Stones and Little Chair Stones to the underground reservoir at the end of the power line. Follow the path to Spoutley Lumb, which has lost its roof, and turn right along the track for 50 yards to the ladder stile on the left. Follow the path along the wall side to the next stile. Cross the next field diagonally towards an electricity pole and descend to a farm bridge. At this point it is well worth making a detour to the left to have a look at Lumb Spout Waterfall. Returning to the bridge follow the track up to farm and continue towards Trawden, picking up a tarmac road at Frighams Cottage. From here it is a few minutes walk downhill to your car.

Walk No 11
Hollingworth Lake Country Park.

Distance 3 miles. Walking time 1.5 hours.
Refreshments: Visitor Centre, or the Fish Inn.

Start point: Hollingworth Lake Visitor Centre. Map reference: SD 940153, marked as a car park on the South Pennine Leisure Map.

Approaching from the M62, leave at Exit 21, the Milnrow turn off (see Map 11). At the roundabout go left, continue over a railway bridge, turn right at the next lights. Then the third left, in front of the Tim Bobbin. Go uphill for 300 yards before turning left to Smithy Bridge. You soon see the South Pennine hills all around. At the T junction turn right and follow the road around Hollingworth Lake, passing in front of the Fish Inn, towards Rakewood. The Visitor Centre car park is 100 yards past the Fish Inn on your left.

Hollingworth Lake was built as a reservoir for the Rochdale Canal in 1804. When George Stephenson built the railway in the 1840's the Lake became a popular inland resort for the Victorians. Today it is the central feature of a country park, with most of the activities that one could associate with country and lake alike. The attractive Visitor Centre has a cafe, toilets, a shop and exhibitions. There are plenty of landscaped car parks with picnic tables nearby and many people spend a summer day close to their cars. However there are several waymarked routes to enjoy, shown on a free map obtainable in the centre. An evening walk around the lake, watching the wild geese in the nature reserve and the sun setting behind the sails of the yachts is very pleasant. There are two restaurants and two good pubs nearby.

This walk starts off along a waymarked blue route, and then omits a rather uninteresting section before ending on the brown route. Once you have the flavour of the park there are endless possibilities for short walks. From the Visitor Centre walk along the track away from the lake towards a gate marked Brearley Farm vehicles only. You are allowed through on foot.

Stop where the track turns right and get to know two landmarks. See how the track crosses a stream and climbs to Brearley Farm, to the right of a wood. To the left of the wood you can see a prominent cluster of buildings at Whittaker. This includes a white house and the Club House of Whittaker Golf Club. Whittaker is on the route ahead, we will climb gently from the left, descend through the wood and come around to join

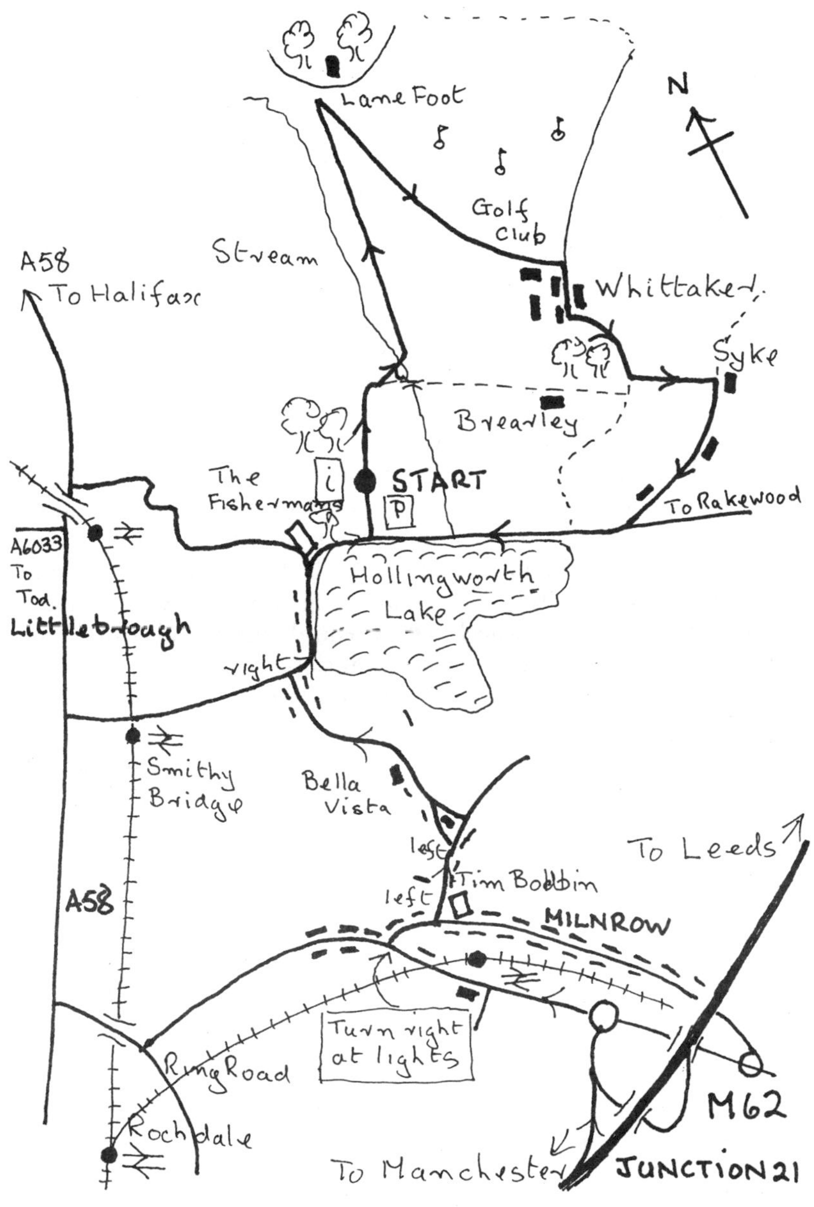
Lane Foot
N
Golf
Club
Stream
A58
To Halifax
Whittaker
Syke
Brearley
The
Fishermans
START
P
To Rakewood
A6033
To
Tod.
Littleborough
Hollingworth
Lake
right
Smithy
Bridge
Bella
Vista
left
Tim Bobbin
left
To Leeds
A58
MILNROW
Turn right
at lights
Ring Road
M62
Rochdale
To Manchester
JUNCTION 21

the Lakeside path.

Follow the path signed to the left, cross the footbridge and go left again over two fields towards a white house at Lane Foot. Just before you reach the road we leave the waymarked route and cut back up right along an old road following the line of telephone wires towards Whittaker. After the gate, the path curves towards the long wall which runs up to the barn at Whittaker. Cross the old goit, taking water to feed the canal at a higher level, and continue diagonally to a stone stile. The next field is a bit of a climb, but it is the last one and well worth it. Keep the barn on your right, pass in front of the club house to a gate into the car park, and onto Whittaker Lane. Turn left into the yard towards a small gate in the left corner. The old house looks ready for restoration. From the end of the yard the view back to the lake and the Visitor Centre is very attractive.

The path goes down through the wood, which is very thin due to undergrazing. To get a wood to grow you have to stop the sheep eating the young trees by putting a fence round it. Soon you see the canal goit again. Go down to the bridge but instead of following the signed route to Brearley Farm, continue along the bank of the goit towards Syke. This is a very attractive building with an interesting stable block. At Syke we are on the brown route. Follow the track to the right along Syke Lane which is made of broad stones for the cart wheels with a central line of smaller stones so that a cart horse can get a grip up the slight slope.

From here you follow the track straight ahead back to the lakeside road. There are interesting diversions around the lake but you are probably ready for refreshments in the Visitor Centre and a look at the current exhibitions before returning to your car.

Walk No 12

Wardle and Watergrove.

Distance 2 miles. Walking time 1.5 hours.

Refreshments: Top Shop, and the Globe in Wardle.

Start point: Watergrove Reservoir. Map reference: SD 912176 on the south side of Watergrove Reservoir on the South Pennine Leisure Map.

Approaching from the M62, leave at Exit 20, the Rochdale turn off. At the roundabout go left towards Rochdale. At the next roundabout follow the ring road signed A6033 to Todmorden. After several sets of lights turn right at the next roundabout, signed A58 Littleborough. As the dual carriageway ends turn left, before the Sandknocker Inn, up Wardle Road some two miles to Wardle. In the village, pass the church an go straight on along the cobbled road, through the iron gates to a small car park at the base of the embankment of Watergrove Reservoir.

Walks around reservoirs have the advantage of being flat with plenty of water in the foreground but they can be uninteresting. This is certainly not true of a walk around Watergrove, there is so much of interest that you feel you want to find out more about the people and houses which used to be here.

The reservoir was built in the 1930's when both employment and water was needed. The people and houses of Watergrove were moved and the great embankment drowned their village. The cobbled road is called Ramsden Road, and once climbed 1250 feet and dropped down a long causeway to Ramsden, which is at the back of Walsden near Todmorden. Indeed the route went on to Burnley via Ragby Bridge, Inchfield Moor, Sourhall, Scaitcliffe, Shore and Mereclough. All this was once a route for pack horse, parts are still a permissive bridleway but it would be good to see it restored as a route for horses.

There are two waymarked routes around Watergrove. We are going to follow the shorter blue route with a little extension. The red route is much longer but with very fine views. Go through the kissing gate on the right and climb the gentle slope to the top of the embankment. As you approach the top, and can see the circle of hills, it is time to get to know their names. From left to right you can see Brown Wardle, Middle Hill, Hades Hill and Rough Hill. The col to the right of Rough hill is where Ramsden Road goes over to Todmorden.

As you go round the corner note the first blue waymarker and then have a look at the wall on your left. It is full of datestones, lintels, mullions and even stone troughs from old Watergrove. One game to play is to find the oldest date stone. I won't spoil it for you but it is well before 1700! How sensible to keep something of the past, but one can't help wondering if the destruction of so many old buildings would take place today.

Follow the road around to the clubhouse of the West Pennine Sailboard Club. If it is a weekend when you go, there will be plenty of members out on the water. North West Water are to be congratulated on making this facility available but it is up to us all to ensure that drinking water is not polluted. As you reach the end of the wall note that the old road, coming down from the right, goes straight into the water.

We cross Wardle Brook and go on to the site of Watergrove Mill, built in 1861, now the club house. You meet the cobbled line of Ramsden Road again as it climbs out of the reservoir. As you walk up the road imagine the houses that were once around you. Note the gate posts which are often the only obvious sign that there was a house or a farm there. Several sites have been investigated and are well worth exploring, try to decide what each room might have been used for.

After the first excavation we turn left across the moor. If you appear to have lost your way, aim for Hades Hill, you will soon pick up the route to another old paved carters road. Note the flat stones for the cart wheels, there will be small stones under the grass between the tracks so that the horses could get a grip as they pulled the cart uphill. A similar road can be seen at Syke (Walk 11), where they are uncovered. Note the standing stones in the field beyond. This is an early pennine method of walling a field, similar to the vaccary at Wycoller (Walk 9).

Turn left down the cart road towards the water, taking the stile on the right just before the water. Notice again this road used to cross the water and you can see the line of it going up the hill opposite. Now we are at the site of Roads Mill, once water powered, with plenty of sites for mill ponds. Some of these will be restored to provide a habitat for water fowl. At post 4 we go left over an old mill pond embankment wall to the outlet. There are still signs of a six inch pipe in the stream bed.

Looking upstream the landscape reminds one of the hushings in Sheddon Valley (Walk 7). If the water level is low you may be able to see the gate posts of the mill owners house, the base stones of machine beds, or brickwork remains. Many of these bricks have markings, I picked one up marked "Withnell Brick 1912". Collecting old bricks can take up a lot of room if you become addicted to it.

Above the mill the path picks up the old road and gently climbs past more ponds up to the next gate. Here the waymarked walk turns left but it is well worth walking uphill for another 80 yards to look at other incomplete archeological excavations of 17th century farm houses. Don't

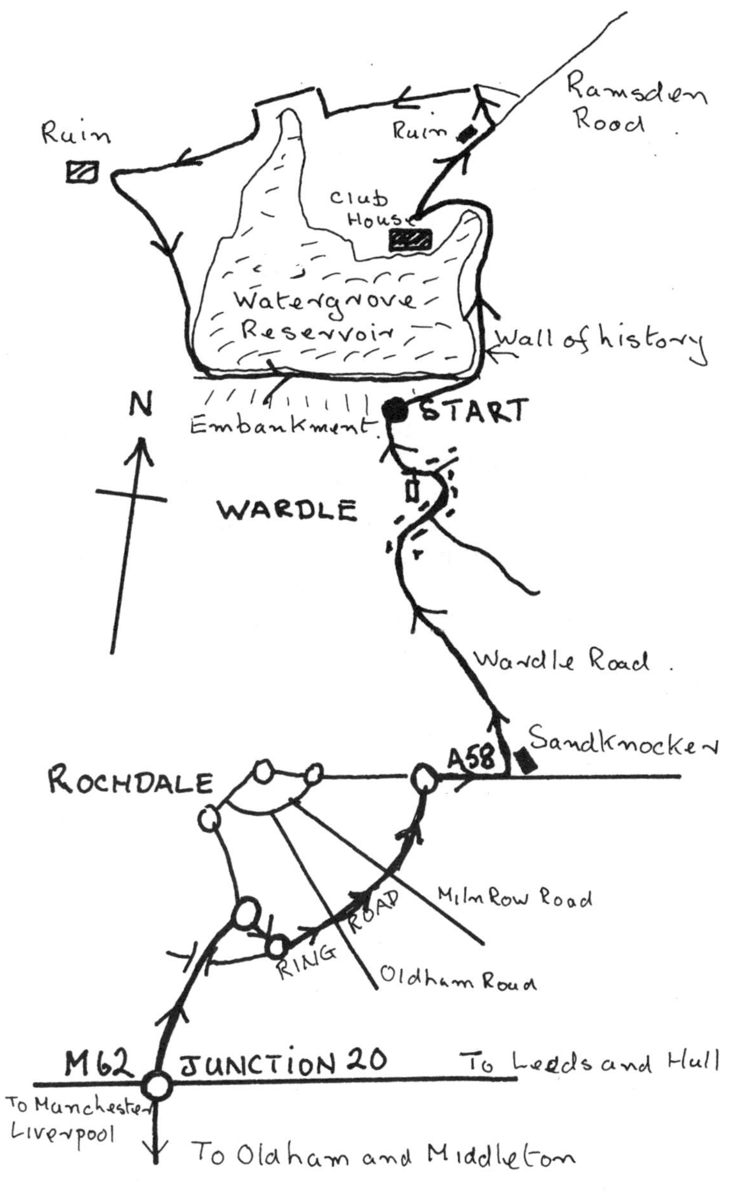
Ramsden Road
Ruin
Ruin
Club House
Watergrove Reservoir
Wall of history
N
Embankment
START
WARDLE
Wardle Road
Sandknocker
A58
ROCHDALE
Miln Row Road
RING ROAD
Oldham Road
M62
JUNCTION 20
To Leeds and Hull
To Manchester Liverpool
To Oldham and Middleton

fall in the well and please don't remove anything from the site. you will soon be able to pick out shippons, mistals, barns, kitchens, and cellars.

Fireplaces were a standard 4 feet to accommodate cast iron grates (18th century AGA's!). Imagine the rooms with their flagged floors and beamed ceilings. The availability of a good natural water supply was one criterion for choosing a building site in the old days. Every farm had its own water supply. The stone vaulted cellars were cool larders. They were always partially below ground and had an air inlet and outlet. The cool breeze evaporated water from the walls producing cooling. There is usually a drain in the floor of the cellar and there are hooks in the ceiling to hang preserved meats. Stone flagged benches had many uses but often carried home brewed beers. Sometimes you can still find gooseberry bushes growing round old farms. These made a good wine.

The path up to Brown Wardle looks inviting and there is lots more exploration one could do, but it is time to take the green road, which leaves the site from the top left corner, down to the blue route around the reservoir. Trees are struggling but the removal of air pollution is now giving them a chance. Any area fenced from sheep will begin to develop its own woodland. Follow the path past the valve house tower, with its 1930's decoration, and cross the bridge to the embankment back to your car. The temptation to cut down the bank should be avoided until a proper path is made. Not only is it steep and dangerous but the Water Authority will not want the bank eroded.

Walk No 13

Callis Wood.

Distance 2 miles. Walking time 1.5 hours.

Refreshments: The Woodman Inn, or Stubbing Wharf Inn.

Start point: Callis Bridge, off the A646, close to the border between Todmorden and Hebden Bridge. Map reference SD 973265.

This is a walk in the woods. It involves a steady climb from Callis Bridge up the Pennine Way. Then we cross an old packhorse bridge over Beaumont Clough and follow the lane, just above the woods, to a spectacular view on Horsehold Crag. Then we have a delightful descent back to the start though the woods.

This walk varies with the seasons. In winter, when the leaves are off the trees, you have a good view through the steeply wooded hill sides of Calderdale but it is wet underfoot, (definitely wellies for the children) and you can be in the shade of the hills. In spring the woods are carpeted with bluebells and wild garlic, in summer woodland scents hang heavy in the air and autumn brings the golden leaves of the beech trees as they say farewell to another season. Whenever you go, you are never far from the sound of streams as they tumble down the hillside.

Callis Bridge is on the south side of the A646, Burnley to Halifax Road, close to the Todmorden and Hebden Bridge boundary. It is 2.8 miles from Todmorden town hall, just after two garages on your right and by a bus stop, stage 17. From Hebden Bridge it is 1.5 miles from the traffic lights by the Information Centre, beyond the Woodman Inn on your right, and some 300 yards after the 40mph sign, turn left over Callis Bridge just before the bus stop.

The road is quite wide at the bottom and there are several places to park without causing inconvenience, but please do not block gateways. As you leave the car you are already on the Pennine Way! The sound of the River Calder will be loud in your ears as it tumbles over the weir behind you.

Follow the track uphill, over the canal, and pass the attractive row of terraced houses on your right. Cross the cattle grid. The sign may say private road but it is also a public footpath. The road zig zags up the hill with a gentle gradient. You may take a steep short cut uphill at the first corner, but a gentle walk to Callis Wood Farm and doubling back to the left will bring you to a junction of two roads. Take the right fork uphill. Above you is the characteristic shape of Foster's Stone, rather like Aladdin's lamp, on the skyline.

The track takes a gentle uphill gradient through the woods and slowly curves to the right, with a stream down below on the left. When a farm appears on the skyline half right, pause to look around. Across the valley you should be able to see the tower of Heptonstall Church and to the right of the church, in the middle foreground, is Horsehold Farm where you will be in a few minutes. Below you, look out for a grass track on the left going down to an old packhorse bridge. There is a large stone in the track to deter folk other than walkers. Cross the bridge, go through the gate and follow the old track to your left. This is Beaumont Lane, now getting very well walked and in need of restoration in parts.

Follow the Lane along the top of Horsehold Wood to Horsehold Farm. As Heptonstall Church comes into view, you reach the cobbled road once used by the horses which hauled canal barges. At night they left the canal and climbed the hill to the stables for a feed or perhaps had an evening grazing in the meadows above the valley, ready for the next day's work. There is a seat just over the wall on your left but there is an even better seat and view, some 250 yards down the road. Take the path through a little gate a few yards after the tarmac surface starts.

This is Horsehold Crag - what a view! Look how the railway, canal, river and road all compete for room in the valley bottom. To your right the picturesque four-story houses of Hebden Bridge cling to the hillside. Opposite the medieval village of Heptonstall snuggles onto the hill top. You can understand why the battle of Heptonstall was won, with its natural defences of three steeply wooded hillsides.

Below left is the Stubbing Wharf Inn by the side of the canal. If you wanted to drop in there for lunch you can follow the canal towpath back to you car. Who would expect to see a level bowling green clinging to the hillside opposite? A few feet to the right of the seat is a circular hole which is used as a post hole for a large cross which is carried up here at Easter. Our path now turns back towards Todmorden keeping a few feet below an old wall which runs through the wood. It can be muddy and slippy here in wet weather. Soon you can divert to the right to see the view from a promontory, the site of a barbecue. The path descends towards the stream. Avoid the broken footbridge and follow the path to the hippins or stepping stones. In wet weather the waterfalls can be magnificent. Over the stepping stones we leave Horsehold Wood and re-enter Callis Wood through a little gate.

The path gently descends through an avenue of silver birch trees - an absolutely fabulous setting if the sunlight is streaming in. It is good to see new tree planting, an activity fostered by Calderdale Council and the Countryside Commission. Soon the path rejoins the road where you may have to divert around stone tipping. Below to your right is the Woodman

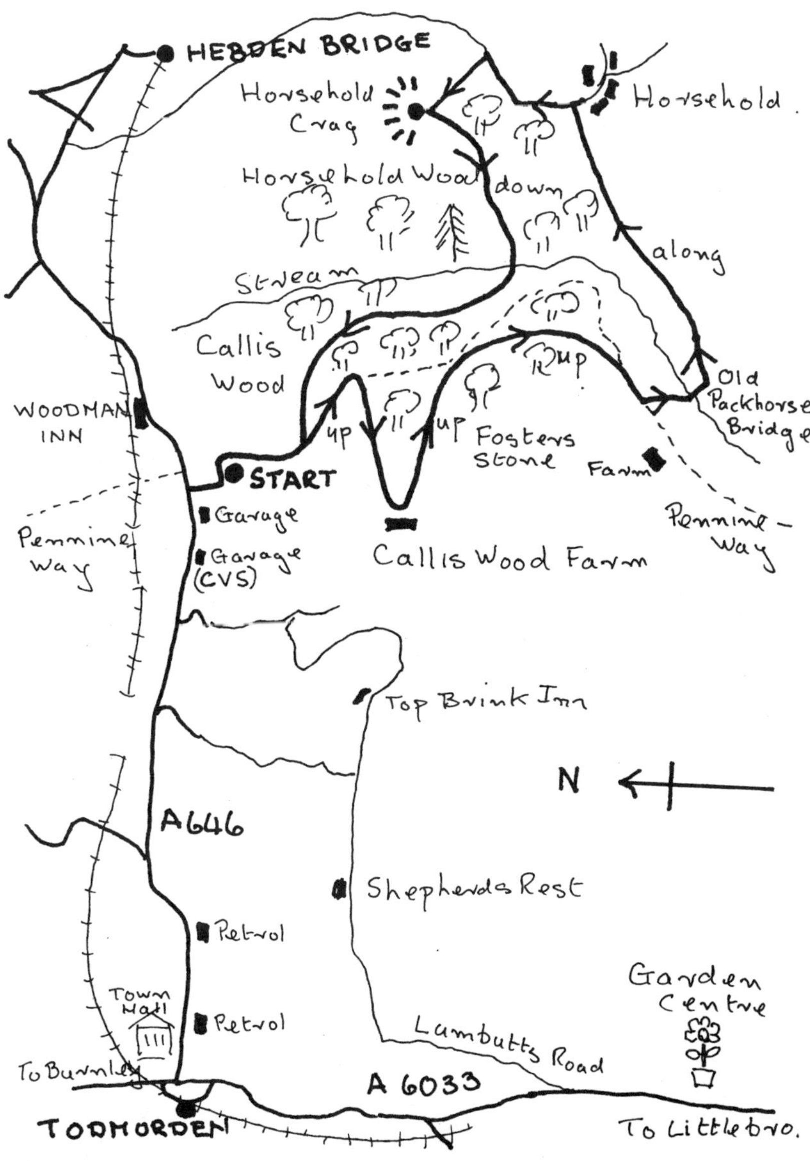
HEBDEN BRIDGE
Horsehold Crag
Horsehold
Horsehold Wood
down
along
Stream
Callis Wood
up
up
up
Old Packhorse Bridge
Fosters Stone
WOODMAN INN
START
Farm
Garage
Garage (CVS)
Pennine Way
Pennine - Way
Callis Wood Farm
Top Brink Inn
N
A646
Shepherds Rest
Petrol
Petrol
Town Hall
Garden Centre
Lumbutts Road
To Burnley
A 6033
TODMORDEN
To Littlebro.

Inn on the main road. It is interesting that there is another parallel footpath below, between you and the canal. This is part of the Sowerby Ramble, a circular strip of land around the old Erringden Deer Park. It is ten miles long and marked in places by the letter S carved into rocks, posts and even houses.

Walk No 14

Colden Water.

Distance 2 miles. Walking time 1 hour.
Refreshments: The New Delight.

Start point: Jack Bridge, on the Heptonstall to Blackshaw Head Road. Map reference SD 962282.

This walk follows Colden Water downstream, mainly along a dry high level route. The return journey is through the woods, where the path can be muddy after rain. There is a popular picnic spot at Hebble Hole Bridge some 300 yards from the start.

As you get out of the car and look around Colden Valley you will see pleasant old farms and cottages scattered about. Our route starts from opposite the top of the New Delight car park, along the bridleway which goes east towards the tower of Heptonstall Church which you can see in the distance.

> Colden water once powered several mills, many of which managed to make the transition from water power to steam power because it was possible to get coal to them. Several chimneys or lumbs as they are called locally, remain in the valley but the mills were small, with no room to expand, and they soon could not compete with the large purpose built mills of Lancashire. The most obvious remains are the sites of the mill ponds, now empty, but you can also see dams, water intakes and goits which carried the water to the wheels. Winter is the best time to look at these remains, when they are not obscured by leaves and plants.

As you follow the track down the valley avoid the temptation to follow the tarmac to the left. This goes to a private house which was once a thriving mill. Instead continue along the track with the river down on your left. Note the site of a deep mill pond just below the road.

The sound of water tumbling over the rocks is very pleasant and you will soon see a clump of trees down by the river on the opposite bank. Look out for a path which goes down to these trees and across a stone slab bridge. This is Hebble Hole, a sheltered spot on a summers day. Here you can watch a procession of hardy walkers, for both the Pennine Way and Calderdale Way cross this bridge.

We cross it too and follow the path to the right for 65 paces. Here the long distance paths divide. We take the right hand Calderdale Way route, signed with a yellow cw, along the causey stones. Note the sites of more mill ponds down to your right which we pass on the return journey.

As you enter the top of Foster Wood look out for the stone stile on the left, some 36 paces into the wood. Once through the stile you can follow the causey stones over three fields in the footsteps of generations of workers who walked to the mill every morning in their clogs. In the fourth field we lose the causey stones for a while. Note how far the river seems to have fallen in a short distance. The village of Heptonstall is marked by the church tower. You can see that the village is well protected from attack on this side by the steep slopes of Eaves Wood.

A new garden is emerging in the fifth field, with new tree planting and waterbaths. Turn right at the end of this garden and follow the track downhill and to the right again at the bottom. This is a Broad Lane, once important but now hardly used. It can be wet and muddy. Continue down at the first hairpin bend but leave the road at the second one, climbing up through Foster Wood again with some fine mature beech trees. Your earlier route is above the wood but now you are quite close to the stream.

As you near the end of the wood the paths divide. If it has been wet underfoot then the right hand path would be dryer, but if the going has not been too bad, the left hand path is more interesting and slightly more adventurous. It takes you down to the walls of the mill ponds you passed earlier and you can see where the dam was in the river and the site of the water intakes to the pond.

This is a place where children often paddle in the summer and some of the braver ones even have a swim. Too cold for me though - give me a deserted beach of a remote Mediterranean island at the end of a long hot summer any time! From Hebble Hole bridge it is not far to retrace your steps to the car.

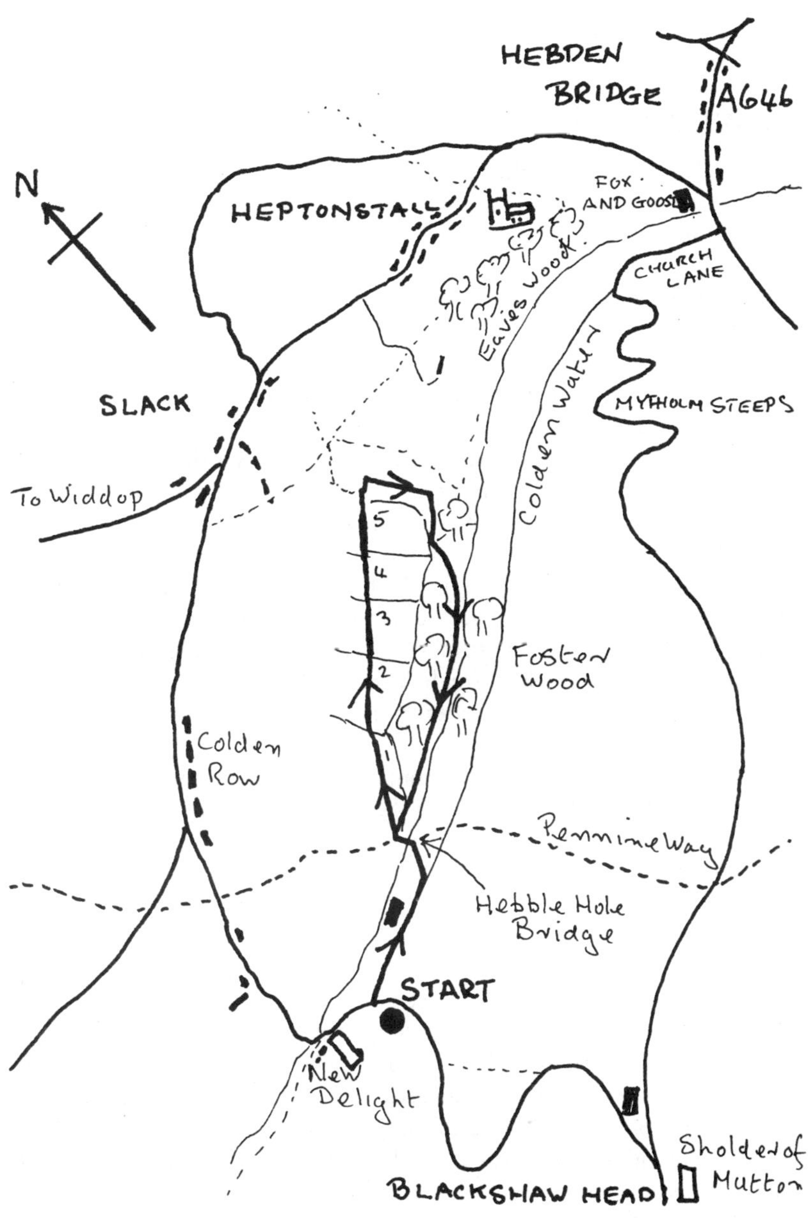
HEBDEN BRIDGE
A646
N
HEPTONSTALL
FOX AND GOOSE
CHURCH LANE
Eaves Wood
Colden Water
MYTHOLM STEEPS
SLACK
To Widdop
5
4
3
2
1
Foster Wood
Colden Row
Pennine Way
Hebble Hole Bridge
START
New Delight
Sholder of Mutton
BLACKSHAW HEAD

Walk No 15
Haworth Moor.

Distance 3 or 6 miles. Walking time 1.5 or 3 hours.
Refreshments: Haworth Main Street is well served with pubs, cafes and an information centre.

Start point: Penistone Hill, one mile west of Haworth. Map reference SE 020365.

Haworth has much to offer the visitor, with its cobbled Main Street, Bronte Museum and Worth Valley Railway, but for me it is the wild moors of Haworth that extend west into Lancashire which are its greatest attraction. The short walk is along the edge of Haworth Moor to Bronte Bridge and Bronte Falls. The optional extension takes you on to the ruins of Top Withins Farm, high on the Pennine Way and the possible inspiration for Wuthering Heights, the Earnshaw Home in Emily Bronte's novel.

Penistone Hill is an old quarry which has been turned into a Country Park with plenty of free parking. The Hill is completely surrounded by road so you can drive around it to choose your parking place, many with spectacular views over the Worth Valley. The walk starts on the side remote from the village, overlooking the moors, so the place near Tom Stell's seat is most convenient.

There is a path over the moor from close to the car park which is best avoided if at all wet. Instead follow the road north to pick up the signed track to Bronte Falls and Top Withins. The appearance of the moor is influenced by the seasons. Perhaps the best time to go is when the heather is in bloom in August but I quite enjoy going with a hard frost on the ground. Sometimes the moor can appear bleaker now than it did in the Bronte's day - certainly more farms have been deserted now.

The first part of the walk is almost a one contour walk. There are gentle undulations but nothing too taxing. The firm track gradually descends to Sladen Beck on your right, a pleasant valley where a bit of new tree planting would not go amiss. The surviving trees have had a bit of a struggle. Bronte Bridge crosses Sladen Beck and the waterfalls are up on your left. This is a pleasant enough spot on a summers day, and you may be content to walk this far and stroll back to your car for the shorter walk.

The route on to Top Withins is more demanding. It involves a climb and the path is wet and eroded in many places - not to be tackled if you are not equipped with good boots, waterproofs, and spare food. You could go half a mile beyond Bronte Bridge where you will be able to see Top Withins in

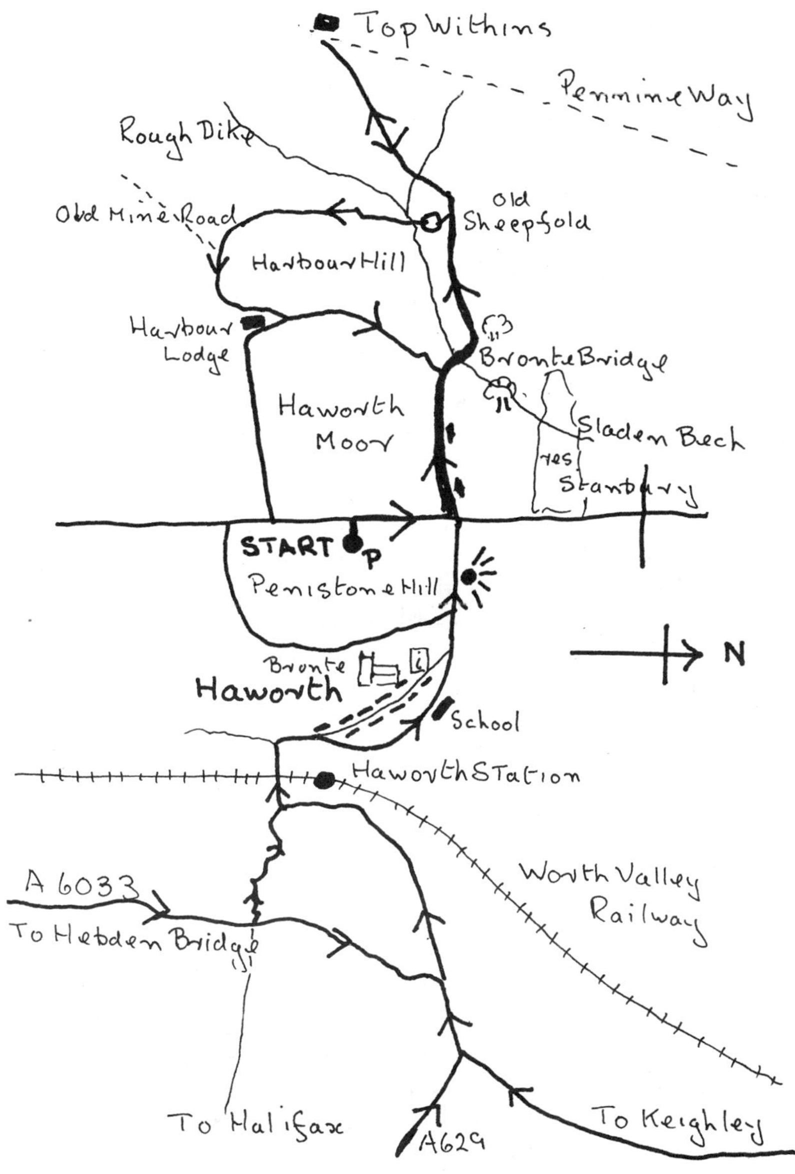
Top Withins
Pennine Way
Rough Dike
Old Mine Road
Old Sheepfold
Harbour Hill
Harbour Lodge
Bronte Bridge
Haworth Moor
Sladen Beck
Stanbury
START
P
Penistone Hill
N
Bronte
Haworth
School
Haworth Station
Worth Valley Railway
A 6033
To Hebden Bridge
To Halifax
A629
To Keighley

the distance and what lies ahead if you decide to to go on.

When you have crossed Bronte Bridge, climb up the opposite side to get out of the valley, and bear left at the signpost to Withins. The ruined farm house above and to the right is called Virginia. It is not easy to make a living up here and if a farm is not easily accessible for conversion to a house it is soon deserted. Follow a well marked track upwards and to the left, running parallel with Sladen Beck going upstream. As you reach a stile in the wall look ahead to a lonely farm, with a tree just below the skyline. This is Top Withins.

The path drops down to the Beck again. You can see the black beds of shale under the moor and the red waters of Rough Dyke joining the main stream. If you go when there are not many people about there are plenty of grouse to be seen and heard. The path crosses the stream and climbs quite steeply towards Withins, where once proud walls have succumbed to wind and water. It is not surprising that both Withins and Top Withins have a good water supply even though they appear close to the top of the hill. These old farms were always built close to water.

The Bronte Society had a stone set into the wall of Top Withins in 1964. This reads "This farmhouse has been associated with Wuthering Heights, the Earnshaw Home in Emily Bronte's novel. The buildings when complete bore no resemblance to the house she described, but the situation may have been in her mind when she wrote of the moorland setting of Wuthering Heights".

There are two routes back you could take but I recommend that you retrace your steps back to Sladen Beck and look out for a path on the far side of the stream. This is close to on old sheep fold at its junction with Crumber Dyke. It is a short pull up the other side to reach a pleasant path which is not as well used as the main path but still obvious on the ground. The moors up here are marvellous, especially when the heather is in bloom. The path skirts the summit of Harbour Hill and as you reach the col, note the old mining road coming down from your right. Go around the hill and pass behind the remote farm of Harbour Lodge. You may hear a diesel generator chugging away, before you get there, for there is no mains electricity out here. Once past Harbour lodge cross the footbrige. You can see a farm road on your right which crosses the moor back to your car at Penistone Hill. This may be a slightly quicker route but it can be monotonous. I thing it is better to take the left path from the footbridge back to Bronte Falls and the Bronte Way.

Walk No 16

Around the Ridge.

Distance 2 miles. Walking time 1 hour.
Refreshments: The Packhorse Inn, Widdop at 978 feet.

Start point: The Packhorse Inn on the moorland road from Colne to Heptonstall. See Walk 2 for directions. Map reference SD 952316. Binoculars are useful for bird watching in summer. Take the stile on the opposite side of the road from the Inn, level with the frontage. Straight away you are on the ridge of land between Alcomden Water, in the valley ahead, and Graining Water in the valley behind the Packhorse Inn. The path goes diagonally across two fields. It can be wet in the first one but thereafter the route is pretty dry.

At the end of the second field do not cross the stile but turn right, following the post and wire fence down towards the road which you join at Holme End where there is a disused barn and cottage. Don't cross the bridge, follow the double track road down to the right. A proposal to flood this area for a new reservoir was defeated in the House of Lords some years ago.

The valley is rich in wild life and even in the middle of winter rabbits scamper about. As the track drops down, the sound of water increases and weathered gritstone rocks tower above. Towards the end of the double tracked road a little gate on the left would allow you to drop down to waters meet at Blake Dean, a popular picnic spot with the children.

Whether you decide to call at Blake Dean or not, your route ahead lies up the main road to the right, to the next hairpin bend, where you take the stile in the corner. Follow the wall on the left for about 50 yards and then follow it downhill for about 25 yards to pick up the lower footpath to the right. This follows the side of the valley for a while and then climbs steeply out of it. Keep your eye open for rare birds, you may see dippers in the river and perhaps a pair of ring ouzels.

Soon Gorple Cottages come into view across the valley with the embankment of Gorple Lower Reservoir to their right. When you meet a low wall keep it on your right. On the opposite side of the valley there is an old quarry where piles of smaller stones are still neatly stacked ready for walling.

The Pennine Way crosses Graining Water, on a footbridge close to waters meet, and it follows the old causey stones as they climb to meet you. Soon you will be able to see the Packhorse Inn across the field to your right.

Look out for a stile, close to the telephone line, and cross the field to the main road and back to your car. The Packhorse is well worth a visit, not least for the photographs around the walls, but please take any muddy boots off before you go in.

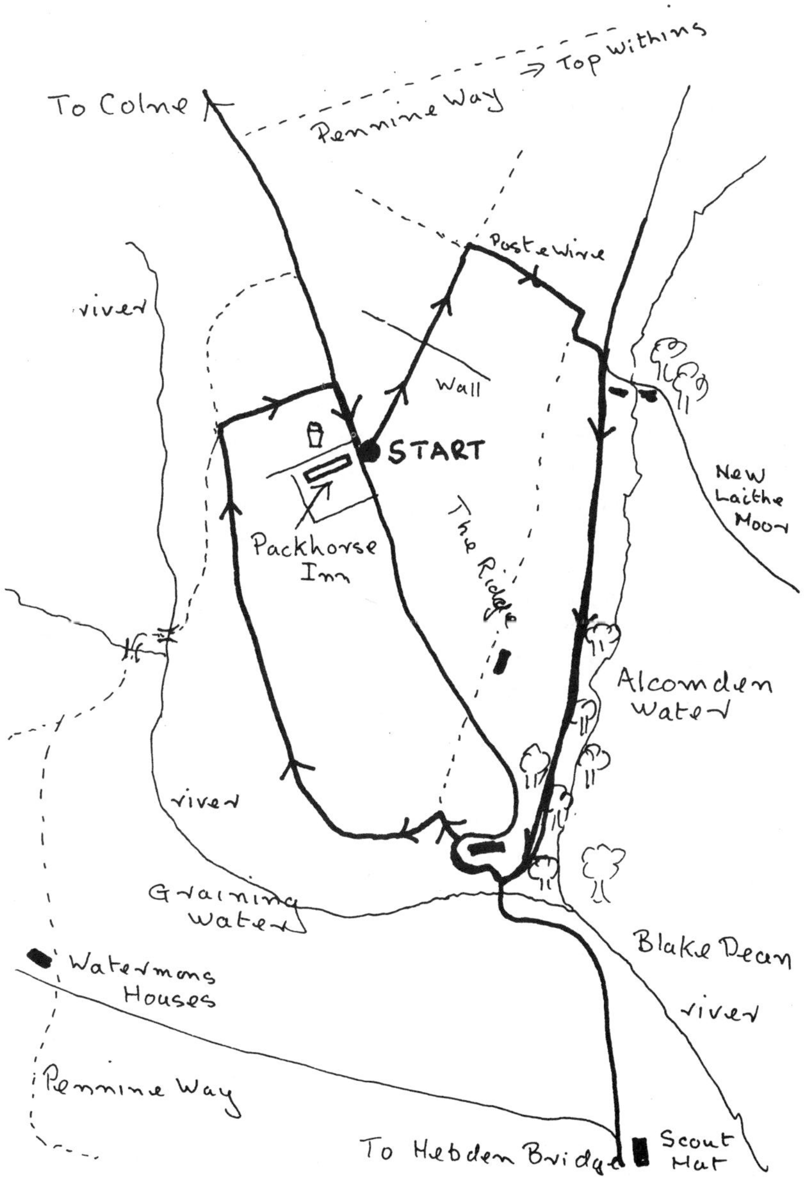
Top Withins
To Colne
Pennine Way
Post & Wire
river
Wall
START
Packhorse Inn
The Ridge
New Laithe Moor
Alcomden Water
river
Graining Water
Blake Dean
Watermans Houses
river
Pennine Way
To Hebden Bridge
Scout Hut

Walk No 17

Widdop Gate.

Distance 2 miles. Walking time 1 hour.
Refreshments: The Packhorse Inn, Widdop, Easter to September.

Start point: Widdop Gate on the moorland road from Colne to Hebden Bridge. Map reference SD 966312.

There is a place where several cars can park, some 50 yards north of Widdop Gate Scout Hostel, just before the road drops down to Blake Dean, but please do not block the Water Board gates.

The path we want to follow is some 50 feet below the level of the present road. There are two ways of reaching it. Either you can go through the gate marked National Trust, Hardcastle Crags towards the seat, and descend 70 steps, or you can walk gently down the main road for 200 yards, looking out for the intersection of the lower path with the road. If you choose the latter route you get a good view of the stone footings in the valley bottom, which once supported a pitch pine railway bridge used to convey men and materials for building the Walshaw Dean reservoirs. You cross some stone flags on the wall to scramble down to the path.

Which ever start you choose, follow the path back to the right back towards the woods. When you are in line with the end of the bridge footings the hillside has been cut out to form a level track for the railway. Now you are on the track of the Blake Dean railway and walking towards the southern terminus at Dawson City, which was next to the road below Slack (Walk 5). The line had a three foot gauge and used timber bridges to cross various cloughs. You can see the stone sides in several places.

The line of the track is level to the first stile, which marks the edge of a landslip. It is possible to cross this with care and once on the other side you can see how considerable the slip was. A narrow section of track widens out into an old quarry. The stone on the edge, with six bolts leaded into it, must have been the base plate for a crane to haul the stone to the track. There are some quite deep fissures in the rocks around here. The railway was dismantled by 1914 so the silver birch trees have self seeded since then.

The line from the quarry crossed another little bridge to a halt with a loop line for trains to pass. This is now a broad path, lined with beech trees. At 5.30am every morning a pilot train would leave Dawson City in front of the "Paddy Mail". When the mail got to the halt it was joined by a crowd of navies who came charging across the fields, leaping walls and clattering along the track in their steel shod clogs. When the pilot had checked the

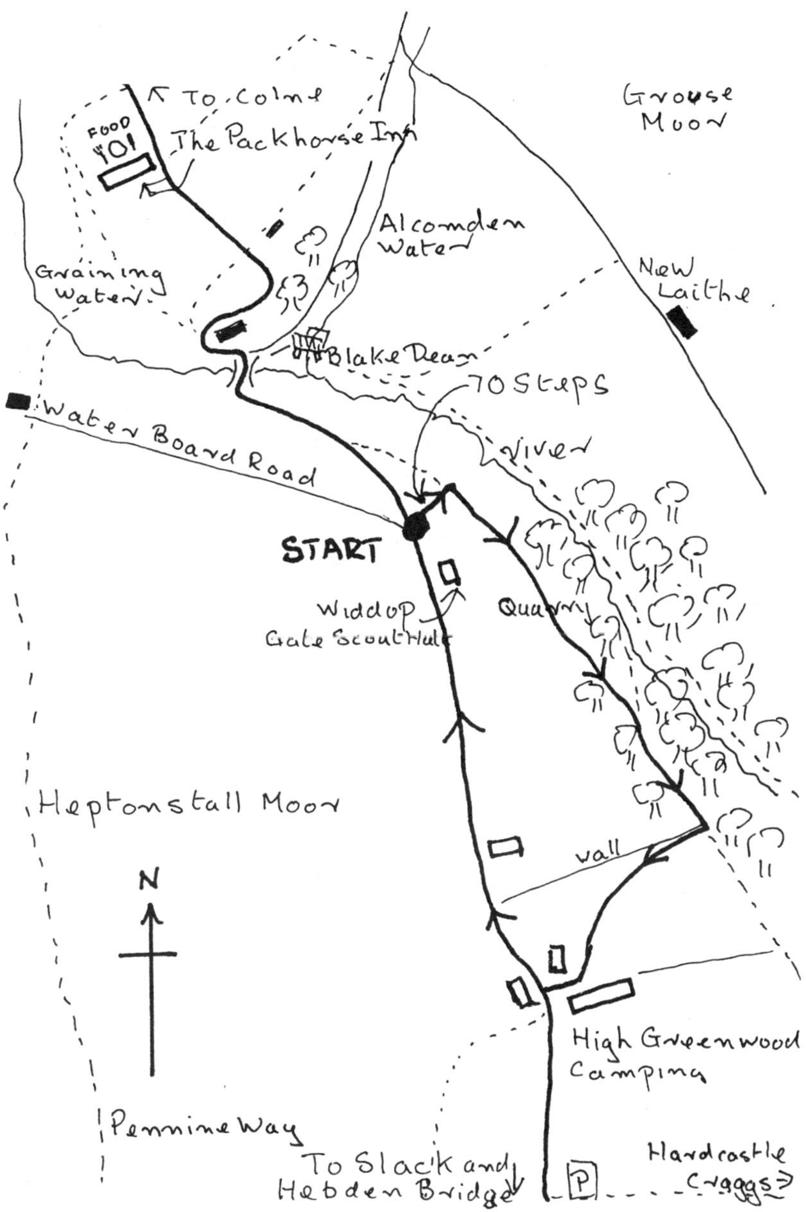
To Colne
FOOD
The Packhorse Inn
Grouse Moor
Alcomden Water
Graining Water
New Laithe
Blake Dean
70 Steps
Water Board Road
river
START
Widdop Gate Scout Hut
Quarry
Heptonstall Moor
wall
N
High Greenwood Camping
Pennine Way
To Slack and Hebden Bridge
P
Hardcastle Craggs

track it would sound its whistle and the "Paddy" would pull away along the hillside and round the curve to cross the Blake Dean Bridge before going into a cutting to climb up to Walshaw Dean.

At the end of the beech clearing we meet another path coming up from behind at a green marker post. At this point the track left the woods to follow a line across the lower part of the meadows above the woods although it is difficult to see the line of the track.

Continue along the same path for another 250 yards and then turn right, next to a seat, up some steps to a little gate. A National Trust sign announces that this is High Greenwood. The path follows the wall half way across the first field and then bears left towards High Greenwood Farm. There is no sign of the railway and yet how narrow is the strip of meadow land between the steep valley and the wild moors above!

The path from the field to the farm gate can be muddy in winter if the sheep have been trampling through for fodder and shelter. Once through the gate turn right along the road when you are half a mile from your car. You see typical Pennine farms as you go, with their barns, or laiths as they used to be called, built alongside the house. Although this road is quiet in winter, it can be busy on a summer weekend, when it is as well to walk on the right facing oncoming traffic.

Walk No 18

Todmorden.

Distance 2.5 miles. Walking time 1.3 hour.
Refreshments: Todmorden town centre.

Start: Todmorden railway station. Map reference SD 936243.

Todmorden is country town at the junction of three valleys. Since 1750, most of the transport routes have been tucked into the valley bottoms, competing for space with the rivers which carved these valleys out of the pennine gritstone. The result is that most people passing through Todmorden never see the marvellous countryside which surrounds these valleys. The town itself is a pleasant place to live, full of history with a thriving community life.

Start with your back to the railway station and walk to the left down the approach road and under the bridge behind the Metro sign. Shimmering aspens line Doghouse Lane as it climbs steeply out of the valley. The second corner is a vantage point to admire many of the historic buildings in the town. Behind the railway station lies the Queen Hotel, built to service the railway. To the left is the tower of St Mary's church dating from 1475, and behind the station is the magnificent spire of the Unitarian Church, but perhaps the most outstanding building is the town hall, designed by the architect John Gibson.

The woods at the side of the road are covered in blue bells in spring and tempting paths lead into the wood. Avoid temptation until you have climbed above the wood and you reach a little gate on your left. The grassy track continues to climb through fields which are full of lambs in the spring. Sheep once provided wool for the hand-loom weavers of the hill top farms.

Bear left at the top of the first field to the stile in the corner. In the second field follow the wall on the left down to a small wood. Avoid the stile just before the wood but take the second one, after the wood. Follow the wooden fence curving up to the left and notice that this path was once surfaced with tarmacadam. The farm ahead is Edge End Farm.

Edge End was once owned by Joshua Fielden, farmer and hand loom weaver. When cotton came to Lancashire Joshua realised that Todmorden's streams could power water wheels so he left Edge End and moved down to Laneside where he set up business in 1782. We will see Laneside later. The business thrived and the Fielden family became very rich, later donating the Town Hall and the

Unitarian Church to the town. Joshua's most famous son was honest John Fielden, a radical reformer and member of Parliament for Oldham who put through the ten hour act. John always remembered how hard he had to work at his loom as a boy. When the new manufactories came along children had to work long hours in appalling conditions. Honest John steered the Ten Hours Act through parliament to ease their lot.

Turn left at the little gate level with Edge End Farm and on to the next gate to join the Calderdale Way along to two track lane. Ahead is Stones Farm. Turn right some 15 paces after the next iron gate and pass behind Stones. As you go notice the standing stones which probably date back to the bronze age. Their location is typical of many Pennine sites which were in use about 3500 years ago.

When you reach the road turn left towards the TV mast where you take the walled lane on the left. This is Watty Lane, a typical Pennine hill road with its old causey stones occasionally surfacing. At the next corner there is a good view over Todmorden to the church tower at Cross Stone. Below you three cottages are tucked into Lob Quarry. Follow Watty Lane downhill for a few yards until the paths divide. We are going to cut back sharp left to the hairpin bend in Stones Road below, but before you leave this superb vantage point it is a good idea to read the landscape.

Note the grassy road on the opposite side of the valley ahead. This is Naze Road, still cobbled but overgrown, another packhorse route leading over Inchfield Moor to Ragby Bridge and then over another Long Causeway to Watergrove, Wardle and Rochdale. In the valley below, road, rail, canal and river interweave continually.

The railway from Manchester to Leeds is the second passenger line ever to be built in the world. The job of carving Summit Tunnel through the Pennines is an epic story and look at George Stephenson's castled bridge below. The Fieldens were directors of the railway company and the quality of the stonework is superb, British Rail should clean the stone, repaint the ironwork and give the heritage of this line the stature it deserves.

Follow the path back sharp left to the hairpin bend in Stones Road and continue downhill noticing the canal locks for lifting barges over the Pennines between Lancashire and Yorkshire. Aim for the spire of the Unitarian Church and pass the gatehouse to Dobroyd Castle. The houses at Laneside, where Joshua Fielden started his business, are now clearly seen on the opposite side of Rochdale Road. Much of Waterside Mill, next to Laneside has now been demolished. Cross the railway and emerge onto Rochdale Road next to Dawson Weir. Walk left into the town centre, through Fielden Square where the stage coach departed from the

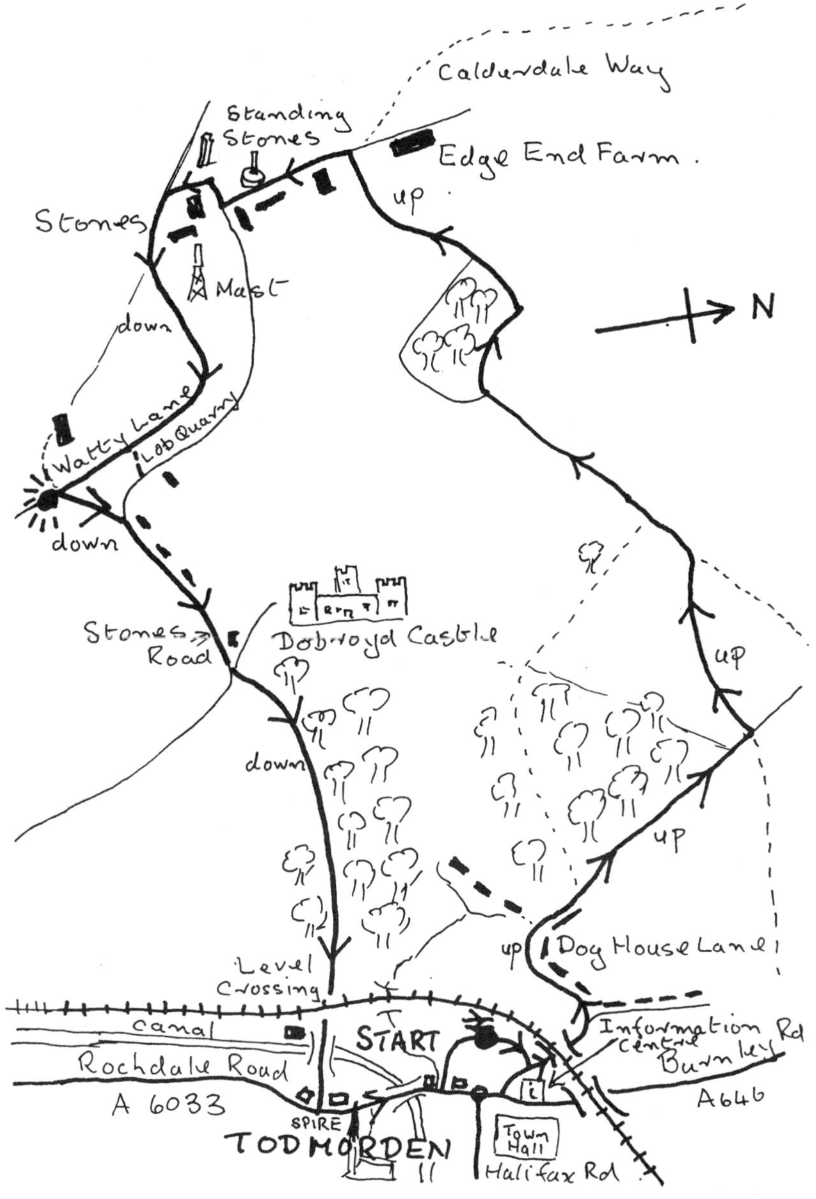
Calderdale Way
Standing Stones
Edge End Farm.
up
Stones
Mast
N
down
Watty Lane
Lob Quarry
down
Stones Road
Dobroyd Castle
down
up
up
Level Crossing
up
Dog House Lane
canal
START
Information Centre
Burnley Rd
Rochdale Road
A 6033
A646
SPIRE
TODMORDEN
Town Hall
Halifax Rd

Golden Lion.

At the canal bridge, pop onto the tow path to note the milestone to Manchester and the ginnel for the horses to go under the road. Return to the road and turn left up Hall Street to go through the grounds of Todmorden Hall to the railway station and your car. Todmorden Information Centre at 15, Burnley Road is close at hand if you would like to find out more about the town.

Walk No 19
Calderbrook.

Distance 3 miles. Walking time 1.5 hours.
Refreshments: Bird i Th' Hand, north of start.

Start: The high point of Calderbrook Road, where a signed public footpath crosses the road, next to an air shaft of Summit Tunnel. Map reference SD 945190.

This walk crosses open moorland and good visibility is needed for navigation. It should not be attempted in mist or snow but on a summers day the moors skirting Allenden Hill and Ferney Hill are absolutely glorious.

Leave the start point by walking along Calderbrook Road in a southerly direction, within a few yards you turn up a double line of causey stones leading off to the right and then follow a grass path between two walls and continue in the same direction when the path becomes a surfaced road. Notice the assortment of windows in the old gritstone houses.

You will soon see a long house at the end of a drive on your right. This is marked Pike Hill on the South Pennine Leisure Map. When you reach the gate at the head of the drive go through it and follow it for about 100 yards, turning right by a hawthorn tree and following the road behind Pike Hill up to Pasture House.

It's a steady climb. A pause or two to admire the distant view of Hollingworth Lake to the south and the old road winding its way up to Blackstone Edge behind you is rewarding. The path passes in front of Pasture House. Keep the buildings on your right and go through a little gate at the side of the wall. Twenty yards on go through the gate in the wall and then continue climbing with the wall on your left.

There is a broad track to the moorland gate. Once on the moor follow the grass track upwards with terrific views over the Lancashire plain on your left. When you reach the stone cairn you have nearly finished climbing. This cairn is your last close landmark for some time, care is needed here, pause and get your bearings. Note the trans Pennine power lines. These can be seen for miles. Behind the power lines to the north east you will soon see the monument on Stoodley Pike.

Take the path to the right from the cairn and count about 125 paces, and look for a path that goes off to the right along the edge of the escarpment. I started to build a cairn at the start of it so add to it if you can! Always keep the edge of escarpment in sight. The danger here is the you will set off across the moors towards Great Hill. The broad pylon, with horizontal insulators, on the edge of the valley should lie ahead for the first part of the descent to Owler Clough Head. Soon you see a wall coming up on your right. Keep this wall on your right crossing a bridge made out of a lorry bottom and head for the largest of the rocks at Ferney Stones.

When you reach Ferney Stones the path turns right and follows the line of a stream and wall on your right towards the large pylon. Its springy turf here and you pick up a line of causey stones when you are level with Reddyshore farm, newly restored, over on your right. Try to walk on the causey stones as much as you can, they tend to disappear under the moor.

You soon reach the track that skirts the edge of the valley. You can return to your car by following this track to the right but at this point it is worth a diversion of 200 yards along the track to the left to see one on the unique pennine milestones at the junction of four packhorse routes. On its four sides it is marked Burnley 9 miles, Halifax 10 miles, Rochdale 5 miles and Todmorden 2 miles - long miles along today's roads. This milestone is not in its original position and it used to be much taller. It was broken off at the start of the second world war to avoid assisting enemy parachutists! At the end of the war it was re-erected on its present site.

Retrace your steps from the milestone, keeping the valley on your left. The Bird i th' Hand pub is below on one of the historic transport routes through the Pennines. You are walking on the original pack horse route from Todmorden to Littleborough. The valley bottom route was a new turnpike road and the charges are still displayed at Steanor Bottom toll house at the junction of Calderbrook Road and the A6033 at Warland. The canal opened in 1804, one barge carrying the load of 200 pack horses, but even this could not service the growing cotton trade so the railway was built by George Stephenson. Summit Tunnel opened in 1841 and was nearly destroyed in 1984 when a petrol tanker train caught fire.

At the pylon follow the track through two gates and notice the causey stones as they occasionally surface. Many a mile of these stones have been buried under tarmacadam but many a mile still survives intact around Calderdale. Take it steady, downhill walking can be hard on the knee joints but you will soon reach the tree line and your car.

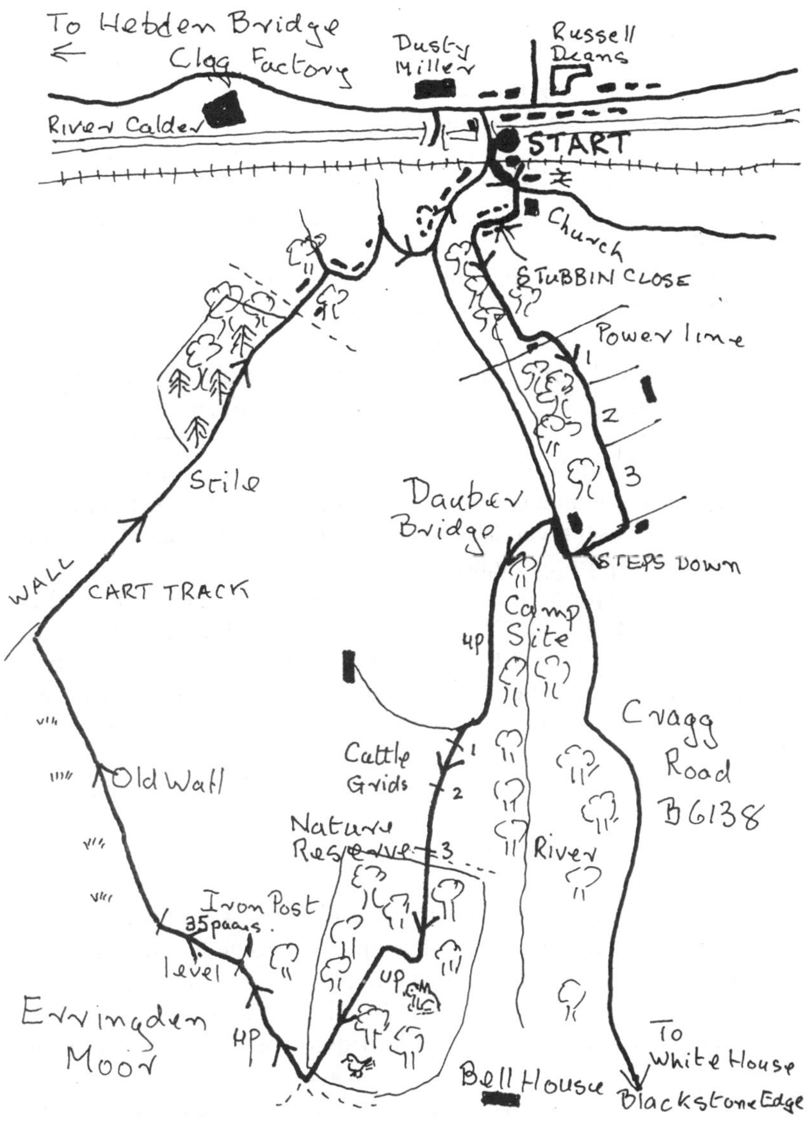

Errata.

The map for Walk No 19 is on page 77.
The map for Walk No 20 is on page 75.

Walk No 20

Mytholmroyd.

Distance 4 miles. Walking time 2 hours.
Refreshments: The Dusty Miller or Walkley's Clog Factory.

Start: Mytholmroyd on the A646 between Hebden Bridge and Halifax. There is a long stay car park just over the bridge up Cragg Vale Road. Map reference SE 013258

This walk has a steady climb alongside meadows before a steep uphill section, through a nature reserve, to emerge high on open moorland. The descent also involves a steep section which can be tricky in wet weather.

Walk away from the traffic lights towards the railway station, rather in need of stone cleaning. Just past the Shoulder of Mutton pub, take the left fork, signed to Sowerby. Go up Hall Bank Lane on the right, by the side of the Methodist Church. Turn right into Stubbins Close and go straight to the end, down the unmade road, to a footpath running between two fences. This is a pleasant woodsy path with a meadow on one side. As you enter the wood keep to the highest path.

When you meet a power line, take the left hand path and go though the stile in the right hand wall. The path follows the wall above the wood, skirting the edge of three fields. Note the pleasant farm house with arch shaped mullions which some craftsman must have built for his lady love. The big stones in the dry stone wall indicate that it is old, pre-dating the enclosure acts.

At the end of the third field, go through the little gate and down a steep flight of stone steps onto the road. Care is needed in crossing at the blind corner. Go downhill for 90 yards, over Dauber Bridge and then take the path signed to Parrock Clough. The sound of water is never far away on this stretch as the path passes a camp site and climbs steadily.

In summer, the smell of cow parsley and new mown hay fill the air in this sheltered valley. Don't be tempted into the woods as you are climbing slowly towards the ridge, ahead right. When the track divides, take the left path crossing three fields and three cattle grids as you begin to see the edge of the moors on the skyline.

At the third cattle grid, cross straight over into the woods opposite. This is Broadhead Clough, a nature reserve preserved by the Yorkshire Naturalist Trust. It is a natural English wood, mainly of oak, silver birch and holly but you occasionally see mountain ash. The route is well made with causey stones, steps and bridges. One hazard you may encounter in

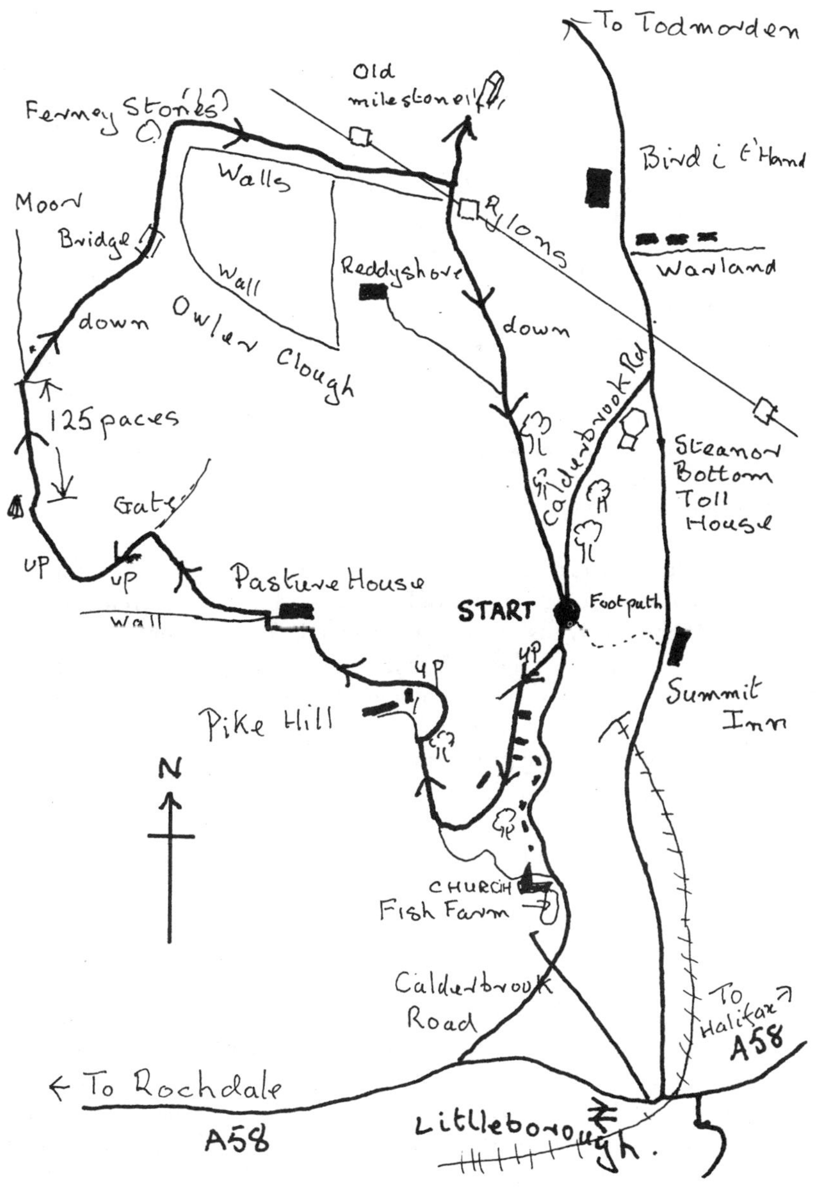

Errata.

The map for Walk No 19 is on page 77.
The map for Walk No 20 is on page 75.

summer are the caterpillers hanging by a silken thread from the oak trees!

You may need a rest as you climb through the woods and it is worth sitting quietly to watch the rabbits, birds and other wild life. it is quite sheltered in the clough, if the day is at all windy, you will be much cooler once you leave the valley. At the end of the wood there is a wooden stile.

The farm on the left skyline is Bell House farm. There used to be a bell here to call the deer in Erringden deer park for winter feed. The park was built in the 12th Century to conserve deer in the Forest of Sowerby but was dispaled in 1449. The boundary is still a public footpath over much of its length and is marked by the letter S carved on rocks.

At one time Bell House Farm was the home of David Hartley, king of the coiners. In the days before gold coins had a milled edge, the coiners used to clip small pieces off the edges and melt them down to cast more coins. The dies have been found in many a local farm and some are on display in Heptonstall Museum. David Hartley was arrested in 1769 and hanged the following year. His grave is next to the old Heptonstall church and his friends carved his name and date on a remote rock at Holder Stones (SD 969216).

Follow the path up to an iron stake, when you reach it you have finished climbing and you are on the edge of Erringden Moor, a fine stretch of open moorland where it is easy to lose your way in bad weather. At the iron stake, with your back to the path that you have just climbed, go forward 35 paces, due north if you have a compass, to the junction of two old walls. The route we want follows one of these walls half right, in a north easterly direction, on the low side of the moor.

In summer, skylarks will be singing their hearts out overhead and curlews will be hiding in the cotton grass. The line of the old wall eventually brings you to a better wall where views open up. You can see the chimneys of Rake Head Farm on your left and the monument on Stoodley Pike behind you. Across the valley you can see straight up Crimsworth Dean. At the far wall, bear right and follow the cart track downhill towards the distant Wainhouse Tower in Halifax.

Go through the stone stile towards the conifer plantation. As you pass under a power line there is a fine view of Heptonstall on the left with the long back of Lad Law behind it in the distance. As you pass the plantation, beautiful Calderdale unfolds. Through the next stile the descent becomes steeper and care is needed in wet weather. At the ruins of Daisy Bank another path crosses but our route is straight on downhill towards the sycamore tree, Europe's largest maple.

The trees become more civilised - apple, cherry and horse chestnut. At the tarmac road turn right, right at the next junction then left down onto the Cragg Vale Road. Turn left towards Mytholmroyd Centre and your car.

Walk No 21
Withins Clough.

Distance 4 miles. Walking time 2 hours.
Refreshments: The Hinchcliffe Arms, Cragg Vale.

Start: Withins Clough Reservoir, off Cragg Vale Road. Map reference SD 986233. From Mytholmroyd, on the A646 between Hebden Bridge and Halifax, take the B 6138, signed to Littleborough, at the traffic lights. Nearly 2 miles up the road bear right down the road signed to Hinchcliffe Arms.

To reach the start from Littleborough, follow the A58 to Halifax. At the top of the hill, past the White House, turn left down Turvin Road, soon signed West Yorkshire and Calderdale, and keep going for nearly four miles. Driving down this road gives you a some idea of the extent of Pennine moorland. Soon after the school sign, take the left hairpin down to the church and the Hinchcliffe Arms. If you reach the Robin Hood Inn you have gone too far.

From the Hinchcliffe Arms follow the road uphill, bearing left at the junction, until you reach the gate of the Yorkshire Water Authority. The Car park is on your right.

When you leave the car park go downhill for a few yards and then take the track that climbs gently to the left. You get the best views looking over the right hand wall. Soon there are small copses on either side of the track. A few yards after the end of the left hand copse climb over the steps set through the wall. Walk up this long field with the wall on your left. Its a bit of a pull and a pause to look over the waters of Withins Clough Reservoir to Holder Stones, the rocky outcrop on the skyline beyond, will give you a landmark seen for miles.

If you are walking in summer the skylarks will be singing their hearts out above you, the occasional curlew and cuckoo add to the pleasure. Little wheat ears flit about close to the ground. Towards the top of the field the monument on Stoodley Pike looks quite large. One feature of this walk is the number of farm ruins you come across.

At the top of the field turn right along the Lane for 100 yards and then left onto a broad walled drovers' road, known as Cragg Road. The high walls can be frustrating for small people but occasional gaps allow you to see the moors. Another farm ruin occurs at a bend in the track. Stoodley pike is looking prominent now and as we walk over the brow of Law Hill the ground begins to fall away. Rake Head is prominent on the edge of

Erringden Moor, half right.

The next ruin is Johnny Gap, 364 metres above sea level, this is a place to pause and admire Calderdale from on high. You can see how it almost folds back on itself. The hill village of Heptonstall is perched on the far edge of the valley, this in turn has been cut deep into the hills by the force of water in the river Calder. Cloud bursts can still produce devastating floods when water, from all the land in sight, drains into one river.

At Johnny Gap turn left up another broad drovers road. This one is some 15 yards wide. You can see the Pennine Way, coming down from Stoodley Pike ahead, where something will have to be done about soil erosion. As you pass the new plantation note the boundary stones marking a line ahead. When the road opens out into an enclosure, follow the right hand wall to the stone stile in the far corner. Now you are on the Pennine Way which we follow south.

A gritstone trough inscribed "Public slaken trough" lies some 170 paces after the stile. Even though it is not far from the summit I have never known it run dry! Many walkers on the Pennine Way walker have slaked their thirst here. At Stoodley Pike you reach the edge and get a terrific view over Todmorden, set at the junction of three valleys.

If you have not climbed inside the monument before, count 39 steps as you climb in the dark up the spiral staircase. Its a good idea to listen for sheep first! From the monument our route follows the edge of the ridge for about 20 minutes walk, giving a birds eye view of the hill villages of Mankinholes and Lumbutts. The square tower you can see, with a central chimney, once housed three water wheels one above the other, generating 54 horse power for Lumbutts Mill. The "chimney" is a spiral stair.

When the path begins to drop, take the left hand path. Soon you drop down to a long leaning stone called Long Stoop. This marks the southerly junction of the Calderdale Way and the Pennine Way. There is a seat, 30 paces to the right of Long Stoop, erected in memory of Arthur Archer, Warden of Mankinholes Youth Hostel in the village below. What a cracking view. You can see Robinwood railway viaduct in the distance.

From Long Stoop we turn left and follow the Calderdale Way all the way back to the car but there is much to see on the way. The causey stones and chamfered waymarkers lead you across to Withins Gate. Just beyond the gate is the Te Deum stone.

Follow the right hand wall until Withins Reservoir is in sight. Some 100 yards beyond the next gate the Calderdale Way has been diverted left, along the contour of the hill. Then it gently curves down to pick up more causey stones which switch through the wall. At the end of the causeys turn right downhill to the track along the edge of the reservoir. If you are lucky you might see a heron shyly sliding away. There were once 17 farms in this

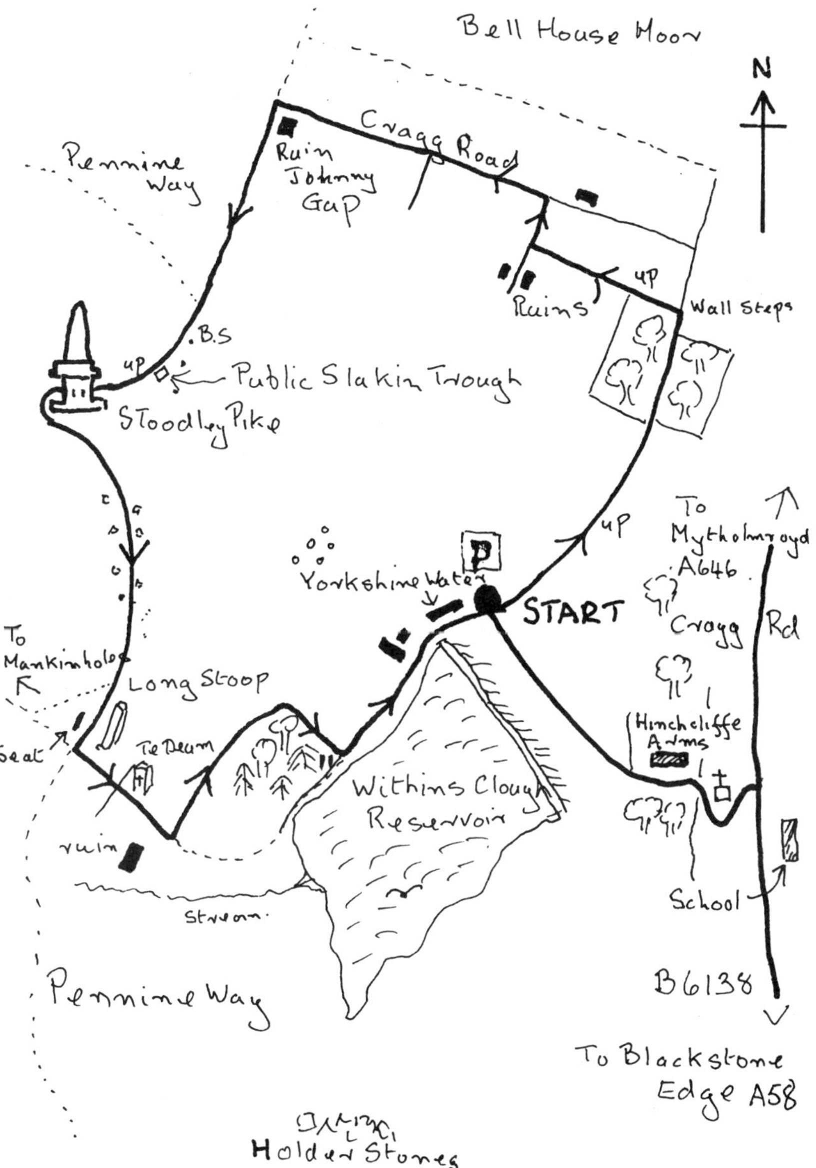
Bell House Moor
N
Cragg Road
Ruin
Johnny
Gap
Pennine
Way
up
Ruins
Wall Steps
B.S
up
Public Slakin Trough
Stoodley Pike
up
To
Mytholmroyd
A646
Yorkshire Water
START
Cragg
Rd
To
Mankinholes
Long Stoop
Seat
Te Deum
Hinchcliffe
Arms
Withins Clough
Reservoir
ruin
Stream
School
B6138
Pennine Way
To Blackstone
Edge A58
Holder Stones

valley, now the only sign is often the gateposts which were too heavy to move. The farms were bought when the reservoir was built for the town of Morley, near Leeds, to prevent water pollution.

At the reservoir road turn left and follow the water's edge. Pass in front of the buildings, keeping them on your left. You soon reach the overflow and the Water Authority Buildings where you car awaits. Please drive carefully down the valley, as there are children about.

Walk No 22

Bride Stones Moor.

Distance 2 miles. Walking time 1 hour.

Refreshments: The Sportsman's Arms, Keb Bridge.

Start: The Sportsman's Arms, Kebcote. Map reference SD 928274. The start point lies on the Long Causeway 7.5 miles from Burnley and 2 miles from Blackshaw Head, see Walk 7 for details.

Park near the pub and walk downhill to the track 150 yards on your left. The name Keb Bridge refers to the old simple stone bridge in the field on the right at the back of the sign to Redmires Dam. This bridge is reputed to be very old indeed. When you reach the track signed to Hudson Clough Farm follow it for about 150 yards to the stile on the left.

The contrast between the moor and the agricultural land on either side of the track is quite dramatic. If you have a dog with you please put it on a lead before you cross the stile on to Bride Stones Moor. Immediately the gnarled and weathered gritstone rocks grab your attention. The broad track lies above the stones to your right. As soon as you are walking on gritstone rock pause and look slightly to you right. Even as late as the nineteenth century people used to live among these stones.

You can see two large parallel slabs of rock sticking out of the ground and the slots which used to carry the roof beams are still clearly seen. the present ground level is well above the original. The house was called Fast Ends (there could certainly be no movement of these gable ends) and in 1810, Abraham Stansfield, one of Todmorden's famous botanists, was born at Fast Ends. He got his education at Shore Baptist School and later lived at Springs, lower down the hill on Stoney Lane.

The right of way does not drop down to Bride Stones Farm, but follows an arc onto the moor. At first the route is defined by tractor marks but, as the ground becomes rougher, aim for a gap in the old wall ahead. The path veers slightly to the left after the gap and gently climbs with the stones and the triangulation point at 437 metres over on the right.

The view from the summit of Bride Stones is very rugged, In winter there are some magnificent sunsets over frozen pools of water giving a very eerie atmosphere. The Bride Stone has a narrow base and is about 100 yards east of the triangulation point.

There are many stories about the origin of the name Bride Stone and two of them were put forward in my book "On the Tops around Todmorden". However a third suggestion has been brought to my attention. We know that this area was inhabited by the Celtic tribes. A Celtic gold Torque, of 400 BC, was found at Cliviger and is now in Manchester Museum. The Romans were always fighting the local brigantes. Bride was a Celtic Goddess, a mother earth figure, from whom we derive our modern use of the word bride. Bridget and Brideh are lovely names and Saint Bridget's saint's day is still next to the old Celtic quarter day, February 2nd. The suggestion is that Bride Stones may have been a Celtic place of worship. This is speculation but there is no doubt that the names of many of our stones pre-date written history.

From Bride Stone the path continues across the moor, meandering towards the far corner, where the distant stone wall joins a wooden fence backing onto Eastwood Road. Turn left along the road for 310 yards looking out for the path on the right which follows the line of a wall on the right across Ingham Pasture, towards a small radio mast. A way marker would be handy here. We are still surrounded by moorland and there will be curlews on the wing.

At the far side of Ingham Pasture we reach the Long Causeway, now covered in tarmac, but a very old route going back at least 3000 years. We know this from the middle bronze age sites. At the far side of the road is a bridleway known as Dukes Cut. At the intersection here once stood Dukes Cross. One of many crosses marking the route from Burnley to Heptonstall. Others are Stump Cross, Robin Cross, Maiden Cross, Stiperden Cross and Mount Cross, which has been moved to a field off Shore Road.

Walk uphill, admiring Bride Stones, now on the left skyline, and note the old milestone signed to Burnley, Halifax and Cross Stone, and on to your car at Keb Bridge. A weekly cattle market was held at Kebcote until Haslingdon Cattle Market opened. Now the Sportman's Arms is a centre for country sport. The Pennine driving club meet here and you may be lucky to see a fine array of horse drawn vehicles. Clay pigeon shooting is a popular weekend pastime in the field behind the pub.

If the walk is too short for you, there in an interesting extension. Take the path to Redmires Dam and following it along to join Dukes Cut. Redmires dam was built to store water for Robinwood Mill in the nineteenth century. It was breached for safety reasons in the 1960s and is now dry. You can still see the remains of tree roots in the far corner, indicating that this area was once wooded. It would be easy enough to raise the bank sufficiently to retain a small amount of water and give the wild fowl a chance, as well as creating an amenity - how about it?

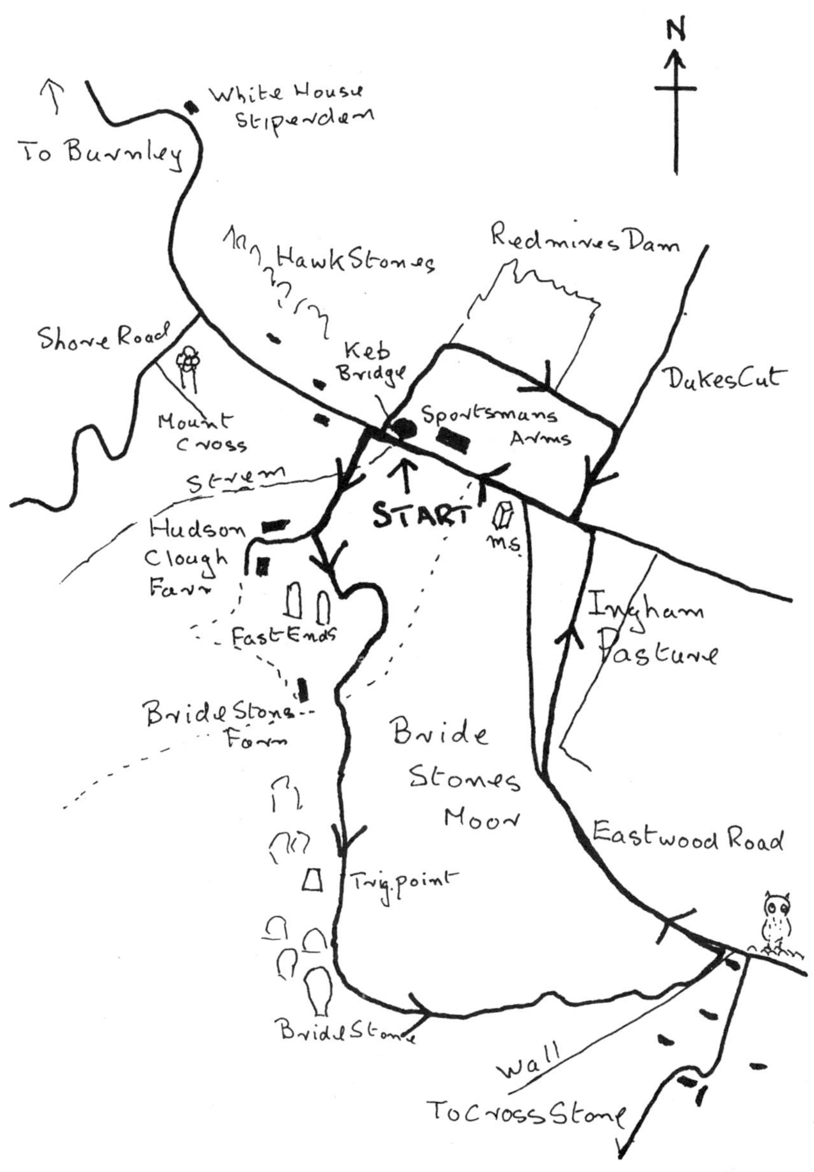
N
White House
Stipenden
To Burnley
Hawk Stones
Redmires Dam
Shore Road
Keb Bridge
Dukes Cut
Mount Cross
Sportsmans Arms
Stream
START
Hudson Clough Farm
M.S.
Ingham Pasture
East Ends
Bride Stones Farm
Bride Stones Moor
Eastwood Road
Trig. point
Bride Stones
Wall
To Cross Stone

Walk No 23

Blackstone Edge.

Distance 2+ miles. Walking time 75 minutes.
Refreshments: The White House, Blackstone Edge.

Start: A Public Car Park on the A58 just below the White House at Blackstone Edge. Map reference SD 968178. The start point is on the A58, 2.6 miles east of the lights at Littleborough, where the Pennine Way crosses the A58, between Rochdale and Halifax.

A car park practically on the Pennine Way gives us an opportunity for two walks exploring either to the north or the south. The southerly walk is potentially more interesting with an exposed section of Roman Road, but the right of way across Blackstone Edge moor is not adequately marked and the alternative route along Broad Head Drain, with a lovely path, does not appear to be a right of way (even though Pennine Way walkers have used it every few minutes for the last 20 years) so we will hike off to the north!

From the car park walk uphill to a point 120 yards past the pub where the Pennine Way leaves the road at a kissing gate on the left. The high bank on your right encloses Blackstone Edge Reservoir. The main use of land land round here is for water gathering, followed by sheep farming and leisure walking. It is level going for most of the way with cracking views over the Lancashire plain.

At the end of the reservoir go through the gate and continue to follow the broad track as it curves along the contour of the hill. Below you lies Chelburn Moor. On the far left you can see The Watergrove Walk, No 12. Just across the valley the highest farm is Pasture House on Walk 19, with lovely open moorland behind it. You can hardly see the valley bottom but the old packhorse route along the far edge is very clear. The valley goes through to Todmorden which is well tucked down below Pendle Hill in the distance.

The trans-Pennine power lines might have been designed as way markers and as you approach them layered rocks of weathered gritstone mark the edge of an old quarry. The path divides at the power line (383 metres) and we take the right track signed to White Holme. The path climbs slightly and we see several rocky outcrops in the distance. Stony Edge, behind Warland Reservoir over on the right, has several natural faces in the rocks and many quarry men left their marks up there. The higher point half left is Holder Stones where the coiners met.

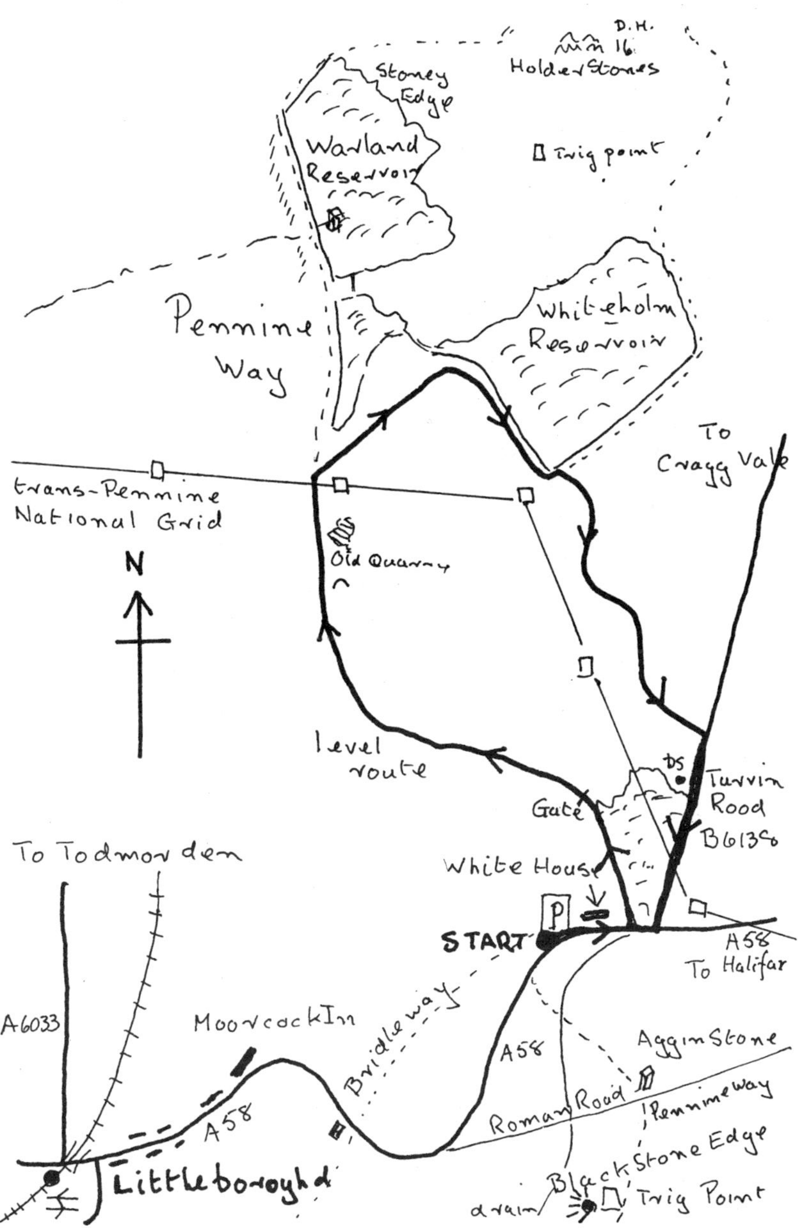
D.H.
16
Holder Stones
Stoney Edge
Warland Reservoir
Trig point
Pennine Way
Whiteholm Reservoir
To Cragg Vale
trans-Pennine National Grid
N
Old Quarry
level route
Turvin Road
B6138
Gate
White House
To Todmorden
P
START
A58 To Halifax
A6033
Moorcock Inn
Bridleway
A58
Aggin Stone
Roman Road
Pennine Way
Blackstone Edge
Trig Point
drain
Littleborough

When you reach White Holme reservoir, follow the bank around to the right to a bridge over an inlet drain. You can see it from a distance as the power lines change direction there. When you reach the bridge take the right track along the inlet drain signed to the B6138, Turvin Road. It will not be long before you can see traffic on it. This road goes down to Cragg Vale (Walk 21) and Mytholmroyd (Walk 20). The hill ahead is Dog Hill, at the back of Rishworth Moor. In summer these moors are white with cotton grass. The drain is nicely graded, aerating the water as it falls and collecting it from every natural gully on the high side.

Turn right at Turvin Road and follow the peat drain to Blackstone Edge reservoir. Note the old boundary stone where the power lines cross above you. You are just crossing from Yorkshire to Lancashire and yet you set off in Lancashire! If you are wondering when you crossed into Yorkshire it was at the high point just before White Holme reservoir. Turn right at the A58 and within minutes you will see the chimneys of the White House, the first pub in Lancashire from this direction.

The White House serves bar snacks and it has a restaurant. Children are welcome until 9 pm and it is pleasing to see really clean toilets. Gourmet evenings are a popular feature here but you may have to book well in advance.

Walk No 24

Cross Stone.

Distance 5 miles. Walking time 2.5 hours.
Refreshments: Todmorden Town Centre.

Start: Lobb Mill picnic site 2.6 miles from Todmorden Town Hall on the A 646 Halifax Road, about 200 yards past a railway viaduct. Coming from Hebden Bridge it is just 3 miles past the traffic lights by the Information Centre. Map reference SD 955247.

Leave the site at the east end climbing steeply out of the valley. Where paths divide take the high one. You soon begin to see landscapes lost to the motorist below. In the hollow below you can see the Arc and Throstle Press at Nanholme Mill where this book was printed.

Soon we reach a cluster of old houses at Rodwell End. This was known locally as ghost town because none of the buildings were inhabited. Now thankfully there is some enthusiastic restoration taking place. The Manor House is on the left and there is a large barn on the right. Go through the stile between the Manor and the barn.

This is a cracking viewpoint. See how the canal, river, road and railway compete for space. The church, half right, is Cross Stone Church, now redundant. This path is well worn as it is used by followers of an earlier guide "On the Tops around Todmorden". Walkers using that will be coming towards you. Note Clough Cottage nearly hidden behind the oak trees below. This is one of many cottages in Todmorden which is not on any public road.

As you round the corner a solitary gatepost has the outline of Great Rock behind it. Great Rock is nearly the highest point on this walk ahead. Turn left at the Lane and after 110 yards take the stile on the right. Follow the wall across two fields, turn right to the next corner and then left. Do not go towards the old farm. The sunken path follows the wall to a stone stile marked Dec 11 1905 T.S. Descend to the stream in Ingham Clough across a natural meadow which is full of wild flowers in summer.

Cross the log bridge and climb out of the clough, bearing right at first then following the line of the wall to the left. We come to Lower East Lee dated to the day, 27 Octo 1631! Much of the property round here dates from round about the same time when timber framed houses were replaced with stone. Many small working farms became non-viable so the land has gone to larger farms leaving the old houses as lovely homes.

We can see Great Rock ahead. There are several routes to it but we will go for a gentle climb. Take the road to the left for 350 yards to the next house. Pass behind it. Don't go through the next gate up the drive to Chapel Houses but take the walled lane to the left. This is little used and gets overgrown in summer. The sycamore needs trimming or it will soon block the right of way. When you are level with the back of the houses go up the steps on the right and follow the contour path through five small fields. You may notice that it is a causey path, but covered over for most of the way.

Soon you reach Eastwood Lane. Before you step down into it have a look at the duck pond. This was once the header pond for the water powered Eastwood Mill below. The feed water to the pond is piped from Staups Dam, to the right of Great Rock above. You could go straight up to Great Rock, but there is a more interesting and gentle climb straight ahead towards the stone barn at Lane House Farm. Note the mullioned windows as you pass.

The track passes two more old houses and becomes a grass track with terrific views down the valley to Heptontall Church and Hebden Bridge. The valley to your right is called Jumble Hole and well worth exploring, but today our route follows the sandy road curving upwards to the left, eventually rejoining Eastwood Lane just below Great Rock.

What a view! The circle of hills from Stoodley Pike around to the right are part of Todmorden's annual boundary walk, some 22 miles long and organised by the Rotary Club. At Great Rock take the road on the left for 250 yards. Turn down towards Todmorden and pick up the Calderdale Way path on your right. Note the quality of the dry stone walling here. It was done by "Action for the Community in Todmorden" or ACT for short. This was part of the Community Programme and when this ended, the last stone, a big one was proudly inscribed "ACT".

You go through two gates and then keep on the level. Do not follow the Calderdale Way downhill. Once we have gained height we might as well keep it, because the view up here is terrific. You pass the new pond at Higher Birks, below left, and then reach the ACT stone, before crossing a plank bridge over the fledgeling Ingham Clough we crossed earlier. The next section of path on the other side was not improved by ACT and what a mess it is. We cross two stiles and emerge on the lane again where another ACT team worked from the far end.

This is a very old route which has been widened at some time. The original causey stones are under the right hand bank but occasionally emerge. Soon you reach a T junction where a bridleway comes down from Lower Winsley. There has been some welcome restoration here by Calderdale Council repairing the take offs, clearing drainage channels and removing blockages.This is a good vantage point. You can see right into Todmorden with the spire of the Unitarian Church being prominent

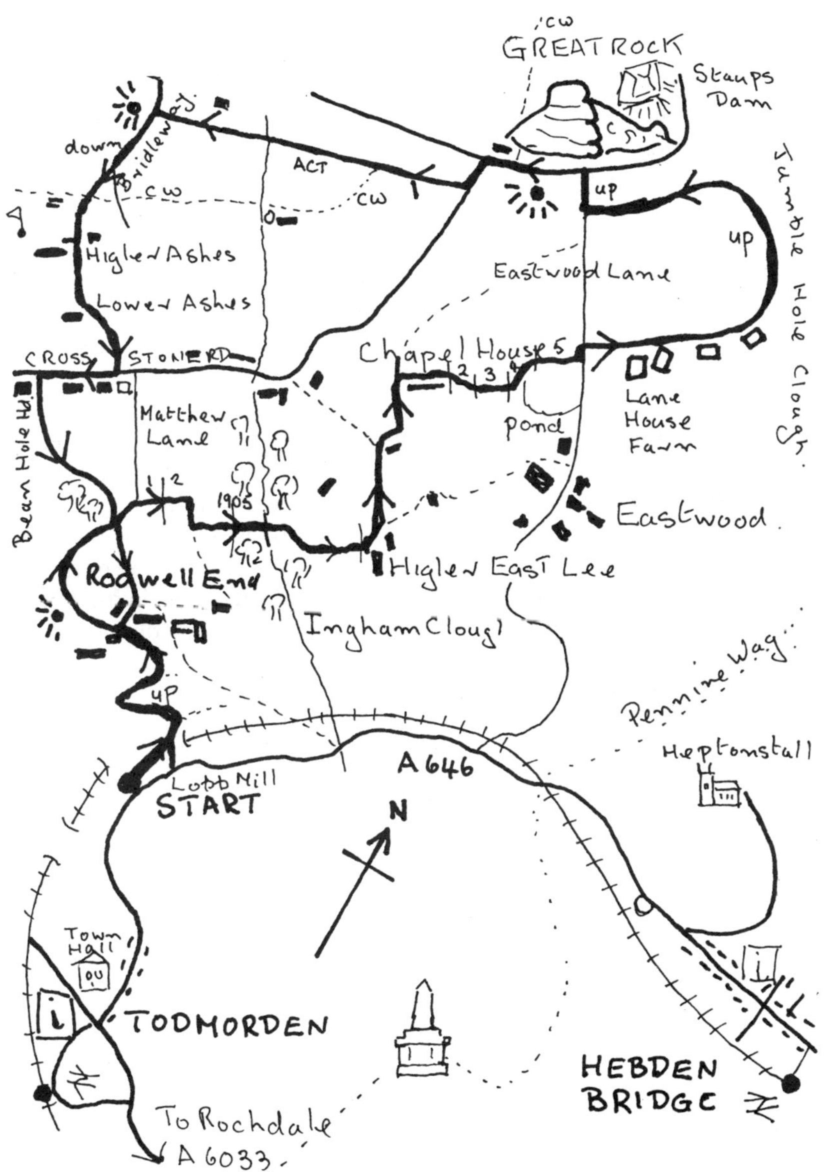
CW
GREAT ROCK
Staups Dam
Tumble Hole Clough
Bridleway
down
ACT
CW
up
Higher Ashes
Lower Ashes
Eastwood Lane
CROSS STONE RD
Chapel House 5
2 3 4
Matthew Lane
pond
Lane House Farm
Bean Hole Hd
1 2
1905
Eastwood
1912
Rodwell End
Higher East Lee
Ingham Clough
Pennine Way
up
A646
Heptonstall
Lobb Mill
START
N
Town Hall
TODMORDEN
HEBDEN BRIDGE
To Rochdale
A6033

behind Todmorden Golf Course, which has a Bronze Age site right in the middle of the 6th fairway!

At the T junction turn left downhill, where the track divides, go to the right of Law Hill reaching a tarmac surface at Broad Ing Top and continue down to Higher Ashes. Turn left in front of the house and note the date on the stable door, I S 1714. This was once a single storey cottage. The next house is Lower Ashes, 1759. Keep left and drop down towards a huge modern barn, which more closely fills the need of modern farming than the older one beside it.

At Cross Stone Road we go right, passing in front of Rodwell Head and Cross Gap, but turn left before Bean Hole Head. When the barn here was converted to a house a fragment of carved stone cross with viking symbols on it was recovered from the wall which may have been the original Cross Stone.

The path heads straight towards Stoodley Pike and now we are getting close to the start. The path follows the edge of the high ground not carved out by the river. Self seeded oak trees threaten to block the path and rose bay willow herb has a go in summer. Clough Cottage is down below again. Soon we reach Matthew Lane and this time we follow it down, turning right just before the remains of Rodwell End Chapel, to pass in front of the huge barn, with its stone arches, before wending our way down to Lobb Mill again. What a fascinating hillside!

Bibliography

Boswell, G., *On the Tops around Todmorden*, Delta G 1986

Calder Civic Trust, *Pennine Walks around Hebden Bridge*, 1989

Calderdale Way Association, *The Calderdale Way*, 1978

Cookson, S. & Hindle, H., *Wycoller*, Hedon,1973

Fielden, J., *The Curse of the Factory System*, 2nd Ed. Cassells, 1969

Fitzgerald, R., *Tempest's Blake Dean Railway*, Railway Magazine, January 1967.

Holden, J., *A Short History of Todmorden*, 1912, Manchester University Press.

Jarrett, J., *The Fielden Trail*, Smith Settle, 1988

Parry, K., *Trans-Pennine Heritage,* David and Charles,1981

Pridmore, E. J., *Fabric of the Hills*, Standing Conference of South Pennine Auhorities 1989

Thornber, T., *A Pennine Parish the History of Civiger*, The Rieve Edge Press, Burnley 1988

Weaver, S. A., *John Fielden and the Politics of Popular Radicalism 1832-1847*, Clarendon Press, 1987

Whitaker, T. D., *History of Whalley,* Vol II, Routledge & Sons, 1876

Index